The Tree Line

THE TREE LINE

POEMS FOR TREES, WOODS & PEOPLE

EDITED BY MICHAEL MCKIMM

First published in 2017 by
Worple Press
Achill Sound, 2b Dry Hill Road
Tonbridge
Kent TN9 1LX.
www.worplepress.co.uk

Printed by imprintdigital
Upton Pyne, Exeter
www.imprintdigital.com

Typeset and cover design by narrator typesetters and designers
www.narrator.me.uk
info@narrator.me.uk
033 022 300 39

ISBN: 978-1-905208-37-1

Legal Sustainability Alliance

The Legal Sustainability Alliance celebrates its 10th Anniversary in 2017 and, as a signature to The Woodland Trust campaign for a new Charter for Trees, Woods and People, we are delighted to have commissioned this anthology of new writing to mark the significant contribution that trees make to our landscape, both historic and current.

The LSA is a network of leading UK law firms who are committed to working collaboratively to take action to improve the environmental sustainability of their operations and activities. The LSA encourages all employees within law firms to work to measure, manage and reduce their carbon footprint and to take action for a more sustainable future. For more information on the LSA, please visit our website at www.legalsustainabilityalliance.com

Contents

WOODS

PEOPLE

Foreword

It may seem perverse, but let me start this foreword with Joyce Kilmer's best remembered, and much parodied, lyric poem, 'Trees':

I think that I shall never see
A poem lovely as a tree.
A tree whose hungry mouth is prest
Against the earth's sweet flowing breast;
A tree that looks at God all day,
And lifts her leafy arms to pray;
A tree that may in Summer wear
A nest of robins in her hair;
Upon whose bosom snow has lain;
Who intimately lives with rain.
Poems are made by fools like me,
But only God can make a tree.

A poet of a hundred years ago modestly downplaying poetry, as a device to praise trees. A perfect introduction, I think, to this fine collection of modern-day poems also inspired by trees. A sylvan anthology to enjoy rather like a walk in the woods - the eye attracted by a variety of shades and tones of subtly different subject matter, style and form: wit and irony intertwined with eulogies, effusions and epiphanies. Here and there are to be found well established luminaries such as Simon Armitage, Gillian Clarke, David Morley and Andrew Motion interspersed with rising stars such as Jonathan Edwards and Helen Mort.

Trees are things of beauty and a joy forever. Down the ages poets have offered up prayers, pagan and holy, to favourite trees; they have mourned their felling and celebrated their survival (Hopkins' 'Binsey Poplars', Cowper's 'Yardley Oak', John Clare's 'Fallen Elm' to take three examples).

Nowadays the importance of trees in the environment looms large in the thinking of the natural scientist and the poet alike. It is not only the odd favourite row of trees that may be chopped down, but whole species ravaged by disease, rain forests destroyed in pursuit of profit, ancient woodlands lost forever. But the pastoral tradition, going back beyond Virgil's 'Eclogues', has always urged city-dwellers to learn from a simpler, truer natural world. As Wordsworth writes:

One impulse from a vernal wood
May teach you more of man,
Of moral evil and of good,
Than all the sages can.

In 2017 the Woodland Trust and other organisations celebrate the 800th anniversary of the Charter of the Forest which restored rights of the ordinary person to make use of woodlands in the 13th century. The 2017 *Charter for Trees, Woods and People* sets out the way forward for our trees in the 21st century.

This anthology reflects our attitude towards trees and celebrates our delight in woodland today, delight Joyce Kilmer would certainly appreciate. In my ignorance, for years I thought Joyce Kilmer sounded like a tweedy old British countrywoman. But, of course Joyce Kilmer was in fact an American man - Alfred Joyce Kilmer. A father of five, prolific writer and volunteer soldier, shot dead by a sniper in the last year of the First World War at the age of 31. And I dare say in his lifetime he thought both poems and trees were lovely. And they still are.

Clive Anderson
President of the Woodland Trust

Introduction

Yesterday I went looking in Epping Forest for what is believed to be the largest and oldest beech tree in the United Kingdom. It's thought to be a thousand years old, and though for the last ten years I have been living within easy distance of it, I only found out it was there in the last few weeks. Editing this anthology, I have started to pay more attention to trees.

The tree I went looking for is a coppard. It began its career as a coppice, the trunk cut low to the ground to leave a stool from which new shoots would grow and be harvested every dozen or so years for firewood. In the 13th Century the coppicing of this particular tree gave way to pollarding, the coppice trunks lopped at head height so each trunk would multiply again and the production of firewood continue higher off the ground. More recently, probably within the last few centuries, this periodic harvesting ceased, and the neglected beech coppard was allowed to do its own wild thing. Approaching it now, around the edge of Lost Pond, last autumn's beechmast crunching underfoot, it looks like thirty trees – from a sprawling base thirty feet round, it rises hydra-headed, sleek and grey and gnarled and knobbly, fifty feet high. Beeches left in their natural state may only survive for three or four centuries, while a managed coppard might survive for several times that. Through centuries of management by coppicing and pollarding, Epping Forest has become a cathedral of ancient trees. As Richard Mabey writes, pollards "are the most vivid demonstrations of what can result from a co-operative between human and nature."

The value of the co-operative between human and nature will be articulated this year with the publication of a Charter for Trees, Woods & People. 800 years ago (around the time our beech tree graduated from coppice to coppard) the Charter of the Forest was sealed into English law as a companion to the Magna Carta, protecting people's rights of access to the Royal Forests. In 2017, on the 800th anniversary of the sealing of the Charter of the Forest, the Woodland Trust along with over 50 other organisations will publish the new Charter. It will articulate how trees and people should be able to benefit each other now and in the future, ensuring that trees are protected and setting out people's rights to the benefits of woodland. To shape this new Charter they have asked the public to share their memories of trees and tell them why trees are important. This anthology aims to complement this work by asking the same questions through poetry: a Charter for Trees, Woods & People in verse.

Over a period of several months I invited poets to write new poems in response to the 1217 Charter of the Forest, to trees or woodland of personal significance to them, or how trees have shaped our society, landscape and lives. The results astonished me. They sent me poems about trees in gardens and along the sides of roads, trees to climb and build dens in, favourite trees cut down. Poems about childhood, memory, history, motherhood, nationhood, law, mythology and death. Poems about turning into trees. Poems about getting lost in the woods. Poems about oak, ash, alder, pine, chestnut, birch and many more besides. They are a profound celebration of trees.

As poems dropped like seeds into my inbox I began to see a structure which echoed the three branches of the Charter: Trees, Woods, People. Although many of the poems could find a home in any one of the three parts, in 'Trees' I have gathered poems in which we encounter individual trees as species or organisms: their life cycles, the pleasure of standing in their presence, the act of taking them apart. In 'Woods' we meet trees en masse, go deeper into the forest and get lost in the beauty and otherworldliness of ancient woodland. A number of poems take inspiration from the original 1217 Charter,

4

soaking up the language, giving us woods haunted by foresters, hunts and pageantry. In 'People' we come out of the woods and witness how trees shape our lives: our culture, our society and our psyche. The poems are at times dark, sometimes painfully sad, and often incredibly funny.

There is also a deep political consciousness which runs through all three branches of the anthology. Most of the poems were written in the latter months of 2016 or early 2017 and it is notable how political events have affected poets' reflections on trees. Our trees and woodlands are under threat from privatisation, land development and the catastrophe of disease. But not only environmental politics: the aftermath of the EU referendum, the refugee crisis in Europe, and the rise of right-wing populism haunt the anthology. In the face of this, trees become a metaphor for inclusion, equality and compassion. But not metaphor only: trees offer, in life and in these poems, a constant and companion, a totem in troubled times.

For me too. Waiting for my morning bus on Forest Lane, busy with school run traffic and the noise from the railway cutting behind, I have become newly aware of trees. Yes, they've always been there, a vague unbreakable presence, but now I have started to notice them individually, to decipher from their winter skeletons the sweet chestnuts, a walnut in the school playground, the crabapples set into the pavement. These poems have inspired me to pay closer attention, to go looking for a veteran beech coppard in my local woods and to plant saplings in a future forest in Oxfordshire. I hope they will inspire you too. And then, upstairs on the 678 from Forest Gate to Stratford, the astounding quantity of trees, once you really start looking: maple and hornbeam and elm and cherry and peaks of planes, thick and full along the railway lines. And isn't it great, that there are so many?

Michael McKimm
London, March 2017

TREES

Thoughts in the Presence of Trees

Trees have more DNA
than you or I.
They have better engineering skills. Look how they hold
    up all those tonnes of trunk and branches
to gigantic heights
for hundreds of years
in calm or gales from East or West, or laden with snow or
    water,
and never lie down for a rest.
Each year they raise from the earth and spill out vast
    waterfalls of leaves
and great troupes of dancing catkins, or perfectly formed
    and intricate flowers,
and later nuts and fruits,
and each autumn they suffuse their systems with
    beautifully coloured antibiotics
that enchant the senses
of an entirely alien species.
We chainsaw them to logs by the acre,
spike them to catch rubber, or syrup,
race up them to gather their coconuts,
strain them against walls to spread out their sweet pears to
    a maximum of sunlight,

and we think they understand nothing!
We think they do not notice
and make no observations about our behaviour.
Sometimes when the forest murmurs
I think they are saying reflectively:
O, fated humanity!
so footloose,
so focused by greed,
so quick to belligerence,

9

so stupidly clever!
You have done us great damage,
but we shall be sorry to lose you –
some of you, after all, loved us.

D.M. Black

Kestanesi

Companioned by eight sycamores at the northern edge of
    the grass,
it does the expected things – silvery bark twisting to the right,
treacled buds at the ends of low dipped branches patient
    through
winter, then open green hands, cream towers of flowers
    bringing
in summer, onslaught of small spiked emerald landmines slung

down on the pavement, splitting, showing horse-flank
    shiny contents
which I pick up and pocket to throw into other open
    spaces, verges
where they have a chance of rooting: smoothly warm in
    my palm,
the perennial gift of autumn, familiar, ordinary; once so
    precious,
mentored into saplings, three foot high, roots swaddled in
    sacking,

hoisted on mules and camels for the snowy winter trek
    from Istanbul
to Vienna – O wondrous tree, ornament of the Ottoman
    Empire,
seen, written of, longed for, by Hapsburg ambassadors,
    guarded and
nursed to maturity in strange new Imperial parks, inkily
    mentioned with
desire and impatience by those further North frantic to
    possess one.

Tree so beautiful it took the temperate world as territory,
    as beauties do,
without effort – by growing, standing, freely presenting
    leaves, blossom,
chestnuts to anyone near: each young one, reaching up,
    driven on by
an old, old memory of their Macedonian mountain
    valley's dappled
light and scent, the singing shore larks – our beloved,
    homesick migrant.

Mary Woodward

12

In the Shade of a London Plane Tree

Sipping tea in your spirit's shade
the kind-house provided for my face
on this hot summer's day –
I wonder about your maple-like leaves
the rings of your age
your spiked fruit-balls
that display themselves like pom-poms
stirred by an inaudible sway of music –
a merging of Oriental Plane and American sycamore –
your hybrid-heart at home in any condition –
winter-dampness or a city's heat-waving pollution –
a hardy Londoner if ever there was one.

Trees – how they intercede
for us, in their green tolerance.

Grace Nichols

The Lime-Tree Year

The ancient lime tree on its square of grass
surrounded by the Physic Garden, the town wall,
the pond with goldfish, the new nursery school
and the library never ceases to give.
In early summer the untattered silk
of its new leaves, curving to points and pinked,
seems to me to be enough happiness
for one person, and though holes soon appear
they only show the tree is doing its job
of playing host to vast communities.
Then come the delicate flowers and their scent.
This July I gathered those and dried them
for an infusion to drink after meals
with guests through the late summer and autumn;
there are some left for the approaching winter.
When I walk there after these thunderstorms,
after these windy days and nights, large leaves,
generously uncrumpled and unsullied,
all a softly bright amber yellow, are laid
thickly over the grass around the bole,
which stands with its bare winter branches now
increasingly disclosed, arboreal
Venus rising from the bath of summer.
It's hard to know which to prefer, the leaves
yellow or green, unfurling or at height,
or the stark beauty of the twigs and branches;
or would be, if I didn't know I don't
have to choose but can move, as the tree moves,
through all the seasons, between earth and sky.

John Freeman

Tree Rings

for Katie at 30

Before the Reverend Goodchild cut them down,
you used to like to hide behind those trees
that outgrew themselves: leylandii.

There were two knot-holes in the larch-lap
where a setting sun would make at a certain point
a kind of devil's gaze. It was a place

to play away the years. And there were others,
some of which we only guessed about,
school clearings, river crossings, or away

in an ice maze or a scheherazade of sand,
where the same tree grew uncontrollably
and the same grim eyes stared through.

★

Sequoia in the distance; horse chestnut candles between;
and close by, the ash, with rose tangled in it.

No bad prospect for a child. You used to hear
doves (and occasionally mice) scratching the flat roof.

There were other noises too, inexplicable ones.
And there below your window, the old woman's well.

★

At the bottom of the garden where now a paper-bark
    maple uncurls,
discarding another draft, there are the remains of that black
    poplar,

the one I proudly tracked down and planted, not the hybrid
street tree from Manchester, but our native *betulifolia*,

of which there are fewer than ten thousand left, or so I
    believed
when it grew into your favourite hanging-out place. The
    swing I had rigged

from one of its three massive stems became for a single
    summer
a glade, a sacred grove to cradle you and your book, until

one night in a millennial wind the whole thing torquing
to itself, groaned, then collapsed across the fence, almost as
    far as

our neighbour's greenhouse. The swing was crushed. I am
    to this day
angry, and thankful, and astonished that such a bough
    could ever have held you.

John Greening

The Elephant Tree

for Elle B

When we go to the park we run
to our elephant tree.
There's a bole in the wood
like an elephant eye; the bark is rough
like an elephant's skin, and the trunk
of the tree dips low,
almost touching the ground.

We sit on it and swing our legs and stroke
our elephant's trunk. We think
we hear him bellow.

Elizabeth Cook

'On the raw shoulder'

On the raw shoulder
        of Royd Edge, the upper limb
of a storm-snapped beech

has ended up wedged
        on a lower branch.
            A little finger

will easily rock
        that two-pronged bough
            in the tree's crook,

but no amount
        of deranged swinging
            can begin to unhook

the dead from the living.
        The winds of the world
            blast and rattle

that private wood,
        and the wishbone rides
            in the tuning fork.

Simon Armitage

How to Take Apart a Tree

The old chestnut is dead. Mossed, bark-stripped,
it must be felled, wind-filled sails brought down,
the tree dismantled, its shadow scoured
from the house-wall, with the mould-grey ghost
sun couldn't reach nor rain rinse clean.

Untie the washing-line where pegged-out sheets
pulled to sea when the wind turned westerly.
Let the rising sun pour gold through un-blind
morning windows. Give the east wind
no instrument to strum on winter nights.

Begin with a branch. The surgeon leans back
from the trunk in his sling and takes it
piece by piece apart with his whining saw
letting each limb fall, the dismembered dead.
Pity the fallen. Trailer them away.

He leaves the limbless trunk to the axe,
gnomon and shadow, standing-stone.
Its populations leave their fallen city,
woodlice, wood-wasps, beetles, ants
bearing their living and their dead.

Respect the old tree's bones, stow log and branch
for winter fires, e-mail the children:
'Your tree is gone'. Spring rains will rinse the wound.
Sunlight will dress the scar in rising grasses,
foxtail and fescue, quaking grass and bent.

Gillian Clarke

Felled

... and after the years of up
and upwards, this: the horizontal
suddenly.
       Stranger still,
this flat face, like no other
dimension I've known,

with all my inside outward,
my interior tidemarks, me
in précis,
       and the whole
stopped clockwork, mainspring
gone... to be replaced

by a different ticking: click
and grind of beetle time,
the gentle
       jaws' attention,
a common-room hush and hum,
their arguments' fine intrications

branching inwards, each
fine-tooled hole that appears
like an insight,
       like an *aperçu*
into the moistening mulch I am
relaxing (I could be at home

here) into. And if Upwards
comes to seem like a diversion
who's to say
            if this is forgetting
or remembering? And why
should I tell you, you who after

all will find out, anyway?

Philip Gross

To my hand-saw's screeching a robin responds.

'It's autumn after summer at last
still little rain but cooling, clouds
won't let fall and birds too silent.
I'm sawing in our blacktop backyard
near a bare garden and small lawn.
The saw's points, no one's oiled,
it must've been left out, I strain
the tarnished blade through once
a riverside branch, tight barked,
no bark really it seems the tree
wore skin, flesh with pulp inside –
its grains and rings cause me to
fall back into origins, memories.

My strong right shoulder aches,
I thrust with my left arm, double-
handed mostly, forcing the teeth –
with broad gaps, closer than some,
I smell the metal and the wood
it almost smokes, almost cries,
recall I should calm my strokes
let the steel's sharpness work
chewing through root and bone.

Long twin-handed lumberjack saw
sometime ripping through brothers
and sisters of the forest, what else?
It's always the same – the burden
to destroy to create – logs spinning
then down sluices. But I'm not there.
I'm (years ago) at one limit of a two

-handed, an eight foot blade with
many wild, like tiger teeth, working
rawing my hands; with another, he's
more experienced in everything, older
but not by that much, once a probation
officer, a social worker, now a co-worker
a house-father, in a growing community
for those with learning difficulties – that
doesn't tell it. It will have to do. I'm there
too, old enough to be given the far handle
'keep the steel moving smooth' the man.
Can't think what the tree had done wrong.

But my mum couldn't bear me in or out
once my dad left. She'd found a better place
for me, than home, she said. Why did dad go
and leave me with this good stranger?

I was too weak but I wouldn't give in
to the giant blade. Heaps of saw dust
under our spread feet. The gentleman
at the other end – pulling as I pushed
pushing when I pulled, back and forth,
hardly in sync enough, but he worried
about me more than the old tree being
brought down. Firewood, I remember,
for the log-hungry hearth in our home.

I lived enough there to be released in
to the confusion of streets, a shared
back terrain, concrete and wheelie bins.
I recall how his worn hands clasped
swallowed up mine (was I child then.
shouldn't I know?) when we finished
the flexing steel rested, then a pause
a creak, the trunk fell hard like a body.

Thump! Boom! Did I once punch someone that hard? The wet sawdust flew up
smattering my face. Trees around here
too quiet, we've killed most of the birds.
I know much, but when I stare into the
mirror at my distorted face, my freakish
stance; or speak with my bitty language
the people, each one looks off or down.
Pity or contempt, not much between.
I know, but won't tell what I know –
we kill the birds and leafy friends
with each killing murder ourselves.
I know that. The cutting edge is stuck.
I make a new groove, from a different
point, hope to join the slashes and cuts.
How deep can I go, before caught again?
I'm murdering the tree a second time,
my old saw blade screeches, screeches,
a nearby perched robin trills a response.
(only know a few, but I know its name)

The soft-handed bloke taught me that,
and how to blister my skin. The robin
why it's so loud, piercing my ears?
He told me – that in everything there's
an unseen, an unheard, that can't be cut.
All things join, weakness and strength,
my craziness and normal people's ways
my saw's bitter sound, a soaring note.

Robin, like nothing I've heard, squeals
and shrills, it must've built its nest
once on this branch, wedged in a crux,
way back through the rings, near the core.'

Paul Sutherland

24

'Reader, allow'

Reader, allow
   the poet to elegize
      the ash:

that bank of saplings
   on Farnley Estate,
      rankled with blight

after two seasons;
   this felled centenarian
      culled with an axe:

on a muted TV
   some Danish backwoodsman
      opens the bark,

reaches in
   through the flaked timber
      and breaded grain,

scoops out
   its pulped heart
      with his pink hand.

Simon Armitage

Forgiveness

'*The infant oak-leaves swung through the sober oak*'
— Elizabeth Bishop

i.

leaf and tree   try   for their first   flower
it has   taken   millennia   to bring   life   to pass
spectra of sunlight astray   seeds   among   grass
their white child blossoms   for a   single hour

leaf   blames tree   tree   blames   the   mother
roots   tremble in beds   listening   to   them   brawl
tree screams at leaf   leaf shrieks at   soil
roots   cannot   tell   father from   mother

all   winter   tree   nursed   infant   leaf
last autumn's leaves   died   incarnadine
come spring tree   tells her   you will wear my crown
tree   is   unfurling   this   lie   all   his   life

branches wrestle for   a   boy's snagged kite
roots   wrangle underground in tests   of length
tree drags water up a   well   of   his strength
leaf is   trying to   be life   yet nothing is   right

tree's canopy susurrates   'we   may   not   die'
that   leaf makes tree   that tree makes grief
that   root   and   branch   shall never know leaf
except   they   will   for   all   trees   lie

roots   rise to their   tip   toes in spate as it rains
drought is white spite   tree is   past   caring
he   stabs   into   soil   steals   water swearing
you have nothing to lose but your daisy chains

26

ii.

two   late   leaves   condemned   to   downfall
they   cling   conjoined   they   clamour   for   life
branch   suckles   seedlings   scarcely   in   leaf
a   trapdoor   bangs   open   and   that   is   all

behold   a   king's   canopy   tree   cries   to   sunset
holds   high   his   crown   drinks   in   all   earth
behind every great tree is   a   great   leaf   stutters   leaf
roots   rant   in   the   dark: *the death of trees is a silhouette*

tree's   mass   executions   erupt   in   autumn
leaf lifts her meek heads   ·   to the hatchet of winds
if tree truly wanted   to forgive our sins
then   why   did   not   tree   just   forgive   them

haloes of tree rings   ignite   under   bark
veins   of   xylem   swell   with blossom and birdspring
tree awakes awakens to   an   ice-   blast   of   song
leaf   light   flickers   on wands   in   the   dark

tree: *grief   makes   you   see   things   that   are   not   there*
leaf: *teach   me   to   breathe   by   holding   to   the   sun*
to hold   *to leaf*
beyond   *the   grief*   *of autumn*

David Morley

27

Some Hope

Ten days away and already
the oak trees have taken the chance
to advance on the house under cover
of the feral grass that once
upon a time was a croquet lawn.

Pushed up pairs of leaves
all over the place. It's the squirrels'
wood, a would-be forest,
growing through what's left of the roof
I look up to, while mowing it down.

Michael Laskey

The Blossom Falls

Standing at the centre of my gaze,
    Insistent,
It was there each time I glanced up from my book –
    The bright white tree.
It beat at the very heart of the window
    With proud, independent pulse
(For it was outside, always outside,
    And never within me).
Loud, it mastered the hot green lawn.

    May blossom tree –
    Emblem of a lustless fertility,
Child of cold mornings early in spring
When pollen floats sadly about the wind's shoulder.
And now, whenever I looked up, unthinking,
The vision exploded once more to my eyes –
    Arrogant in its virginity,
    Extravagant in its purity.
Finally, transfixed there, I sat through the spell.

★

    I walk along the road,
    And the wind is blowing
    Blossom from the trees.
    Scraps of flickering white
    Drop noiselessly about me –
    Sometimes singly;
    Sometimes in crowds
    They fall.
    I know that wind, I think.

★

I looked out of the window suddenly.
I noticed a very ordinary green tree
    Flecked with dry brown.
        My proud tree,
    The garden's bright lady,
    Had been ravished
        Joylessly
By the blood-red tongue of time,
Which rolls round and round
    And round in its lapping.

        I admired you,
        Poor little tree,
        When you rose alone,
        Untouched by the garden,
        The child of unsinning.
        I resented you then –
        May I say it, my friend?
            I pity you now
        As you cringe at the sky
        And wither, absorbed
        In that stretch of rich grass.
        And your sadness is mine.
            Poor little tree.

Joanna Seldon

Tree in the Garden

Amanda bought it a decade or so back
from our local Woolies before it shrunk
to The 99p Store and we were never sure

if it was an alder but it's come on
from a stave sheathed in cellophane
to something with a trunk the girth

of a telegraph pole, that Alan-a-Dale
or Will Scarlet might hide in before leaping
down on a meal ticket from King John.

It takes from the undertow of traffic
down the London Road, gives its pick
and mix shadows, like Pissarro in Norwood.

Peter Carpenter

Song of the Retail Park Tree

All day, the sun umbrellas outside Café Nero
mimic me. I am bought
en masse from a gardening supply store
in the Midlands and will be paid for
in 36 easy instalments. My watering schedule
is outlined in the staff handbook. My roots
do not go deep. Somewhere, in an office in the city,
there is a version of me
in blueprint. Here, a gull harvests
french fries from a McDonalds carton
on the pavement in front of me
and cries. Nobody will ever carve a heart
into my trunk, my bark. No one will ever
pick fruit from me, in this, in any, weather.

All day, the awning outside Subway flutters
its eyelashes at me. I am background,
atmosphere. I am freezing
my tits off. The kid who plays
peek-a-boo behind me
is called off by his mother towards
Iceland. Somewhere, in an office in the city,
a slightly greener version of me
flickers on a screen. Sometimes,
the wind runs a hand through my hair, but mostly
tired people sit on the bench in front of me
and smoke. I shade
no lovers. No birds will ever build
a nest in me. Nobody will ever call me home.

Jonathan Edwards

A Redwood

I am now on the inside. There is no stench of burning
though the hollow is dusted black and it smears
my fingers with powder, last motes of the fire.

I pick at the walls with a nail, draw strips
as pliant and hardy as dollhair. Outside

your footsteps circle the trunk, they resound,
they are making the fallen needles shift at my feet.

Through lightning and wildfires, droughts and acid soil,
a redwood thrives: two thousand years old and still young.
A rustle – and through the split bark, you climb in beside me.

Swithun Cooper

Brinsop Poplars

Coming away from the party a moment
we rounded the outside of Brinsop Court
and crossed the little moat into the carpark.
There was a wall of trees in front of us,
grey poplars in a single lofty row,
so old I could not think or wish them taller,
nor sturdier, nor more gnarled or musical.
I tilted my head back and found I had to
tilt it again to see the end of them,
the swaying tips of the trees against the sky.
How the little leaves all up and down them
flashed lighter and darker green in the stiff breeze,
while their collective whisper like the swish
of water over many million stones
in a rocky cove made a peaceful roar,
a sound more quieting than any silence.
And how each filled the spaces others left,
though still with air and light round every branch.
In that wind while the boles of the trees seemed
not to react they must have flexed and braced
down into their roots as their tops swayed
in a co-operative, each single leaf and stem
obeying the unseen force in its own way,
but with a harmony perceptible
as tops which bent as far as rootedness
would let them one way bent back with the tension,
following examples set around them
in movement neither uniform nor random.
All the time the motion of each leaflet
solicited the eye, its voice the ear,
and though I stood more than a tree's length off

I seemed to be enclosed and taken up
into their company like a tree myself,
standing there long enough to feel I knew
what it would be like to stay forever.
You rejoined me, and we rejoined the wedding.

John Freeman

Tree Time

No, no. I'm not angry you're late.
See, I just happened to notice
this entire hillside of trees –
maple and oak mostly, and tall
also, maybe sixty / seventy-five
feet, standing close together
from the road-shoulder on up
like a well behaved crowd on bleachers,
waiting for a parade – and fell
to marveling what it could be
they *are* waiting for, held there,
each trunk to its shackle of turf
for life, and none the worse for it,
shimmering and swaying in fact
as if trumpets and kettledrums could be heard
already... and – well –
it is hard to conceive
(as I guess we're supposed to) that,
seen from a tree's viewpoint,
there's no view and no point; that
despite the enormity and duration
of the enterprise, a maple or oak
doesn't know it exists, let alone
how many decades it's waited.

Or are we too little, too
hurried, to grasp so great
a magnitude of anticipation, so
millennial a patience – though
not unmoved at the thought of it?

Peter Kane Dufault

The Ashground

Where I found my place
but mistook for The Ashgrove
in yonder green valley.

    And mistletoe
    wiped off the beak of a thrush
    in the high branches
    then darkly multiplied.

Where I lay beyond my own sight
in a nest of leaf-mould
and luscious bluebell clumps.

    And the pallid flap
    of elderly children
    living too slowly
    too far from the light.

Where I began to understand
the conversation in whispers
between root systems of neighbours.

    And lightning conducted
    through sleek rainsheets
    streaming without a break
    from flashpoint to base.

Where I decoded messages
crackling out to growing-tips
diverting them round tricky stones.

And fungus shrouds
unwrapping their cottons
or driving in a wedge
of sick rubbery ochre.

Where I heard gallons
eased from the sweating ground
squeeze up corridors beneath the bark.

And the trees replete
with their surplus of light
manifest in gold leaf
cast down and consumed.

Where I saw the swaying crowns
exhale an endlessly blue sigh
into heaven as it tumbled by.

And the wintry lop and echo
of ash after ash after ash
tossed from solid ground
to blaze in my head.

Andrew Motion

Alders

We swam in the river from a dense alder wood
called Cloven Carr. At dusk we would relight
our fire in its cold stone circle with ease,
and bake potatoes in embers. Charred, hot,
flaky skins, white and exquisite within,
barky and buttery. I still taste them
whenever I smell alder, leaf or bark, still see
those embers whenever an alder is cut.
Then, as the cut turns bright orange the memory
opens out into summer sunsets emblazing
the red-bloomed boughs and leaves, and setting in
the musky, wild scent of the trees and the river
as it flickered and burned above its stony bed.
We did not know that alder made charcoal
of intense heat, that it created the weapons
of the Celts. We found and lived the knowledge
without knowing. In such a way we knew
alder thrived by, was hardened by water,
using it as a ladder into and out the current,
with shivering, dappled flesh, green with dye
from trees that loved their element and with which
we felt affinity. Since then, I have loved alder
and its place in the world, its purple cloak
in winter, warming larches and the dark boughs
of oak and ash, complementing the grey of beech,
the fine outline of linden, and providing
material upon which red-sprigged birch
threads silver. That last year, I swam the Usk
in March, on a dare. The Carr was level
with the swift, deep water. I made the leap,
swam three strokes before the current overwhelmed

but the alder branches leant, I grasped
and heaved my numb body to the cheering bank.
It was the final time, though I did not know then,
that I would feel that river flowing through me.

Ruth Calway

Spruce Sonogram

```
                                          but        calm
                                          when
                                          sun        me
                                          shines
                                          my         black-
                                          presence
song      wet       black-                like       birds
of        weaves    birds                 an
spruce    of        swirl                 alarm      muffled
soars     leaves    swirl                 flies      moss
high      trailed                         up         and
and       webs      of                    tender
sweet:    of        above                 tawny      you
me        sound     ground                bark       can-
unseen              sound                 strokes    not
in        in        jaunty                           say
morn-               as                    calm       you
ing       head      a          shook      the        don't
mist      of        shanty     shook      tree       believe
```

this
is
a
living

thing?
only
just   more
                                    absent
now   fingers   from   eyes
sentient?   webbed   the   drip
even   with   clouds   the
Darwin   dew   but   light
said   eye-   kept   of
root   lashes   in   the
tips   tipped   the   spruce
act   with   leaves   the
like   rain   inches   sound   soft
the   less   held   from   the
brain   leaves   here   my   light   spruce

Elizabeth-Jane Burnett

Midland Hawthorn

First, the words desert
us. Without the twitter stream
of swallows on lines, eager
to be away but pregnant
with the promise of return.
Instead, this slow slipping
into silence, dwindling specimens
stumbled on somewhere
with little or no fanfare.

Acorn, bluebell, conker.
Now my timeline tells me
these too, and more, have been shed
by the Junior OED, replaced
with others sprung from soil fresh,
solitary, interior, virtual.
LOL. You can't love
what you can't name.
So, let me learn you now

that I might better care.
Let me look beyond leaves,
glossy-green and three-lobed,
the early promise of snow-dust flowers
that quickly turn to cadaver stench,
beyond berries, bright
along ridgeway and drove road,
the blood of the many
who wandered beyond words.

Remind me again how those haws
hide twin seeds. One that grows
to thoughts of long-gone heath
and purlieu, acres once wide with
the language of survival. Agistment,
estover, pannage. Another that lies deep
and hangs on, while winds whisper
what still might yet be.

Matt Merritt

Tears I Shed Yesterday Have Become Rain

After Thich Nhat Hanh, at Trees for Life, Dundreggan Forest, Scotland

in low boats of cloud harboured in the tree-ringed mountains,
in the Bracken, Ling, Bell Heather that cling to bare peaks,
in ancient Oak, Scots Pine, Aspen, Alder, Birch,
in purple Blaeberry juice staining our hands,
in a burn's icy milk charging a gorge,
in gilded clarity of pools –
tears I shed

in boggy trickles,
red hairy Sundew, Butterwort leaves
spread like skins of small, green bananas,
in Meadowsweet, in Orchid, in dusky yellow stars
of St John's Wort, in a Birch stump with Polypore hard
as granite hooves, in the Dragonfly perched by the loch,
in people replanting the Caledonian Forest – tears I've shed

in Red Squirrel, Pine Marten, Crested Tit, in spewed guts
    of a Toad
crushed on the road, in tourists pedalling through the glen,
in the Water Avens' claret petals, in the Moriston's
broad expanse, in snouts of Wild Boar
rootling on its banks, in Harebell,
in Eye-bright –
tears I shed

in Foxgloves
nodding by the wall, in fairy
horns of Lichen, pale as snuff, in the dawn
mists encircling the yurt on this day
of my departure – tears
of the Great Heart
pulsing in all.

Helen Moore

WOODS

Fathoms

Walking inland, sand in the seams
of my coat, salt crusting
the one bent hawthorn of my thoughts,
                              I looked up

and saw myself standing among trees.
                              I had forgotten
that the world could be so vertical,
        that there were pressures that could hold
things upright against the wind.

I knew that water, hurling itself against rocks
could catch the light and hold it mid up-shoot,
but I had forgotten that water and light
could fuse into such solidity.

To stand in rockpool stillness and hear the tideline
in the sky.

I have lost my bearings before, been turned
by a heavy break until I no longer knew which way was up,
but to walk here,
                where depth runs the horizontal axis –
I had forgotten all of this.

And even though I could already see the limits
of the tree line –
                a buckled wire fence
                the herring bones of fields –
I emptied my pockets of coral husks, plastic tags
and bright white stones
                        and laid a trail
against forgetting my way home.

Ben Smith

On Entering Duncliffe Wood

What is it the wood keeps to itself?

Some story of Domesday scribes, po-faced,
foraging for stinkhorn and death cap?

The words that rooks overheard
of Cromwell's so-called parley?
                              A tale
of abandoned babies perhaps, here
where the stumps and roots are draped
in a plush of moss and look more
like the claws of dragons.
                              Or is it to do
with the nuns, how they spoke
of the shameless fern unfurling its bishop's crook?

The twitch and stagger of the beech tree's
dangling rope, is it that?
                              I tell you –
a few steps in and your heart will start
at the crack of a stick, at the woodpecker's
echoing 'knock, knock-knock',
at the creaking tree, the distant shriek.

Stephen Boyce

The Homecoming

for Petrov Zalienko, the Hermit of Hendy Woods

Hold your breath. Still yourself. No twig-snap must break
the spell so pick your way with flattened feet, your measure
of the mossy ground. Is this the way you remember it?
Heavy horizon; reeds skirting the water? Long-limbed
silhouettes of trees shift into focus. Their fingers raise the sky,
uphold the quiet and dank: leafmould, woodsmoke.
You hear the coots' grouching, low honks in the measly light.

Imagine bringing your dogs, your pigs if you had them,
snouting for tubers. Hoik yourself up into an oak's fat arms
and survey the land. Settle snug in the crook. You're invisible
again; your bones snug against the bark. All the king's horses,
all the king's men ride by in their pickups, radios cackling.
Their headlights strobe the mulch into cranked-up
daylight. Later, you'll scout for bilberries, cobnuts that rattle

like broken teeth. You'll whistle back at the herons' croaking,
purse Tor-grass between your lips. That ship you came in
     on, the iron
sea – gone now. Blanks in time. Gunbarrel. Sallowface.
     Your bones
cringing in the rusty hull. What crisis? Here's a half-shelter,
lean-to. Here's your kettle-smoke, your hearth. It's
     morning already,
and the embers are still puttering on. Your skin
thickens up. You can feel it ossifying, gnarled as ash-bark.

Your scalp's a muss of twigs. Your limbs? They could
     easily web
into roots, or grasp into roots. Your feet grow glossy and
     limber, drink

53

the underground mumble of fungi, carbon, hormones
   seeping like song.
Gulp down this snapshot: woodsmoke, leafmould, heavy
   horizon.
Is this the way you remember it? Reeds skirting the water,
   long-limbed?
You're home. No twig-snap must break the spell, so pick
   your way
with flattened feet. Still yourself; hold your breath.

Kate Potts

Wyre

Hawkbatch

Here frowning goshawks bend the tops of pines
with their heavy nests, set their eyes on the undergrowth
where rabbits hold back until sunset.
Ants struggle pine needles across the trails to vinegar nests
through the ruts of walkers' feet where the mud
is the same colour as last year's fallen leaves
as if, worn down, one could become the other.

Callow Hill

Round the back of the visitor's centre is the step
where I used to sit on your break-time
Saturdays with a hangover and a piece
of carrot cake balanced on a saucer on my knees
ten minutes off from trawling the freezer
for the mud-streaked cyclists: *Cornetto, bab?*

Pipeline

On the map the pipeline splits the green
like a printer's mistake.

These windowless brick structures
that house the valves
formed my childhood assault course
but when I climb them now
it's not for a game of *Gladiators*

it's to hear the rushing
of Welsh water underneath,
73 miles without a pump,
striding out to Birmingham
only the gradient making it go.

Deer Museum

Its corrugated shed-ness housed scenes
of taxidermied bodies found on roads
and in woods. A dusk owl on a branch
mice in the dry grass like balls of dust.
Next door were the papery foldings
of adder skins in drawers, a shelf
of unborn fawns in jars of bluish liquid
increasing in size, the largest almost ready
to walk out of there on its pin-sharp hooves,
the white spots on its coat the size of pennies.

Button Oak

Browtine, baytine, traytine, palm
someone still knows every deer in the forest
by its head, and they'll keep telling it till the forest's gone.
Used to keep a book of drawings like a who's who
no need for it now. It's a delicate thing to see one
stepping from the bracken at dusk, head up
all parts working together, the two of you
inside the evening, until it catches your scent.

Suzannah Evans

Shadow's Shade

River Crowdundle, darkling and flashy
below the acorn bank, glances up
through the oaks' twisting limbs,
finger-flutter of ash: water-light
skims off the leaves' late-summer
sheen across tall wings of shade.

Deep among roots, between here
and somewhere, Ross buried Shadow,
by a secretive river flinging a zest
of sunlight off its sidle and scurry,
while leaves seemed to hover overhead
quivering on windless currents.

He scrounged cobbles from the stream
to drop in the hole and keep from scavenge
that bundle of love, bone, old tartan rug
and shaggy fur brindled like leaf-litter,
before he infilled it with loam and dragged
a boulder across for guardian/gravestone.

He is shade himself now in the woods
he husbanded, while the dog, woodwise
and nosy in their ever-after-life, slips
through water-light, leaf-light, questing
hither and whichway between here
and nowhere through their tangled haunts.

Linda Saunders

Regarders of the Forest

fluffed in frost, a robin sings high up
                    as sun low down
                    lays down on draggled moss

while at our feet below the chestnut bough
                    the emptied chestnut cases hedge
                    & hog through leaf mould

here step the beasts of the chase, namely
                    the buck, the doe, the fox
                    the marten & the roe

this day in Sallow Coppice, we are late-come
                    regarders of the forest,
                    witnesses of waste
                    & assart, purpresture

here's forest law, protect the vert, protect
                    the oaks, protect the lesser trees,
                    the hazel, elder, sallow,
                    on which the deer may feed

it's late December, & the deer fruits nibbled down
                    soon, at our snapped twigs
                    the does will lift their heads

& turn long eyes to stare
                    then rise to run, their pelted
                    shoulders touching
                    as they flit this wood

the wandering court brings justice

                for offence against the venison,
                the dog-draw & the stable-stand
                the back-bear & the bloody-hand

now here's neat underwood of birch & ash

                all stashed between the boles
                of coppice stools
                & toppled fern not frozen back

there's bleat of hungry sheep

                four fields away
                & cars hum
                all around this wood

while under soil the Saxon Mocktree Forest

                surges below Weo Edge,
                beneath Stoke Wood
                it leaves a trace

old hunting ground that noses down

                the Onny, scents along the Teme
                & runs the hart
                through Bringewood Chase

Jean Atkin

waste, assart, purpresture: offences against the 1217 Charter of the
Forest. Waste was the clearance of land, assart the creation of new
arable and purpresture the enclosure of newly assarted land.
deer fruits: berries, seeds, nuts
vert, venison, green-hew: the forest, the deer of the forest, the trees
wandering court: the forest eyre, an itinerant court to enforce the
Charter of the Forest

Forest Diptych

Charter of the Forest Wife

I'll have honey out of his forests,
my soft bed made from feathers of his falcons,
eagles, herons. I'll have the brushment borne on his back
for my fires, spin greenhue cloth to fashion
his ranger's garb fifteen days before the hunting of deer begins
at the time of the year's third Swanimote.
I'll have the pannage, fee-farms and asserts of a bride.
I'll lie with my verdurer in the forest.
No abbot, prior, earl, baron, justice, sheriff,
or bailiff a better man than him.
Married law of the forest joins us.
Give me the Honour of Lancaster,
it would not outshine our realm of oak and ash,
holy as where we were joined at the church door,
forest customs being our liberty and state,
as the far-away king,
who makes legal bridges over legal rivers,
has said in the book of this land's fate.

'Forget not the corbie's bone, put it high up on a tree'

I have the raven's fee, the flinty-eyed eagle's kinship,
the hawk of May for my brother.
I have place-names of England for my leafy companions.
Boar's last breath and stag's split windpipe honour my blade.
My knife's friend to no one, foe to all, even a king of the
    English,
though I bear the four hard seasons for him.
His script (they say) is gracious towards forester
and haunts of game, speaking the rights of thicket and
    green purlieu,
when to whip the hounds, how to break-up the deer for
    best gain of the good flesh,
numbles and haunches to the lord, neck and chines to the
    vassal,
to the forester the right shoulder of the beast. Which I know.
They say the ink of the writing is blue or black, not green.
I've heard the tallest oak cry out in anguish to the shining axe
and so I would not boast myself against the crown.
You and I will be who we are, Wyf, subject to all folden
    law, and our own love tokens.
Here's our fox-skin bed, and a merry night to us!
We who can neither read nor write, like the green saints of
    the woodland,
keep their saint-blessing, for we do their biding before we
    do the king's.

Penelope Shuttle

61

Waves

There are children in the trees.
High above the day's parade,
Lichen at their fingers and scraped knees,
They wade

Into the skyline and the green.
Children looking down have seen
Grown-up faces hidden by the waves,
Have been

Like churchyard children at the graves
Of commoners and dignitaries
Who played,

Lichen at their fingers and scraped knees,
Up above the passed parade.
There are children in the trees.

William Wootten

The Royal Forests

In the royal forests, the chimera was idling
by a mirror pool, calm as a self-driving car.
In the royal forests, my breath moved slowly
against the pile of my blue velvet snood.

Lichen was lime green and frilly, as it clasped
the oaks' new growth. The scar of a cut branch
would burst in spring into a brown firework.
It was all starting again, the dynasties, the cooking:

game, and jugging and spatchcocking
in the quasi-taverns skeletoned in gold wood.
Light pooled in certain places, and from others
it kept away, like indigo around a wax resist.

I hurt my hand in the royal forests:
a splinter got wedged down behind my nail.
For a long time I didn't realise, about the birdlime
and the stage set, and the twinkling.

I didn't realise that the investment,
and the visiting henchmen were incidental,
that it was about the bark, and the water
ascending the tubes in the trunks' rinds,

that it was about the trees, not the haunted air
that peopled the gaps between them.

Judy Brown

Twisting Out

A wood knits things
    together, combs rain
        and wind, condenses

a green net catching
    itself, the riddle
        of twigs losing us

eyes scattered
    to slow wounds,
        ash furrows, oak hawsers

unpicked and tipped
    by winter light,
        a birch's witch's broom

a brain the bird sings in,
    has sung, summer's
        bird silence pulsing

in a pendant fuzz
    of twig and mulch.
        A few leaves open/close

yellow in breath
    otherwise undetected,
        the woods frost-locked

graining to dusk
    around crabapple halos,
        green stump trig-points

and the sweat
    of not knowing
        where you're going

the path looping back
    to the stream now
        flowing the wrong way

deja vu of its cold
    weight sounding
        under green sails, yes

green now,
    for the small epic
        this returning without

prospect is through
    the valley, each call
        a point apart and within

a voice twisting
    out, humming
        the same tune over, over.

John Wedgwood Clarke

Oncology – Ethie Woods

'tree-in-bud': *a linear branching pattern of spread of tumors into other areas (radiopaedia.org)*

★

the trees are light:
a physical disturbance
a whirling of mirrors

here in the now
and everything is motion –
sycamore, alder

crowding together
in flickering leaflights
in ferocious whispering.

★

beech and oak, standing
like hymns in the forest,
single cells drinking in the sun

a slow transfusion
in the upper layers –
light into matter.

★

Spring:
like the greening of a lung,
cloaked in its own

bright fur
of wet, lucent spore,
beady, microscopic –

its metabolic
spread in all directions.

★

a tree grows out of itself:

lung, sap, root
the white embryo
muscled, curling under

leathering,
the nub of its joints
bulging like iron

the whole blind process
unfinished, beginning
again and again.

★

suddenly, the wind floods in –
a headlong rush
of branches, like children

playing hide and seek
finding holes and tunnels,
burying insects.

★

sun.
an all over warmth
opens the petals of her body

her sessile leaves
growing bright and pale,
slanting outward

the dried buds
the dark callus tissue
yellowing in sun spots

the seeds of her eyes
deeply enclosed.

★

the blackbird:
its sideways glance,
its upwards listening.

★

as if this was a room in a house
the furniture all gone, the ceiling lifted at last
the light falling in

herself dead centre
ushering in guests, who whisper in monotone
cirrus   cirrus   cirrus

★

a hurricane, trapped:
whitish, like thunder
spilling and slamming

in disbelief, routed
clashing the pines
their roots ballooning;

credulous holdfasts,
hurling and hurling
in colossal abandon.

★

all afternoon
in small, even rain
the birch, eavesdropping.

★

the half life of insects:

charged particles,
spinning in small collisions
as they fizz and hum, unwinding

each brief iota
tingled, nasal and keening.
their thin harmonics.

Lesley Harrison

beetles

upturned chafer
stops

last crank in black
chassis

stops
japanned mechanical

legs
unable to right the red–

black
varnish never couched in

text or
journal as it sinks through

anonymity
a single tiny ship to mulch

eggs – last–
ballast eggs never known to

entomologist
as the crew kilometres away

put polish to
idea: their eco–mentary here

that closes
with long-shot mist to fore

-ground
clearings where soil must

breathe
shallowly — not as it did

when growth
meshed soil to canopy

yet it
whispers frequency

no circuit
finds *When the*

last tree falling
falling

falls
there will be

no one
to hear it

Mario Petrucci

The Grace of JCBs

Spring detonates on time thanks to wood anemones.
Woodland is wan without a million of them.

JCBs squat on fly-blown, gull-flocked hills.
They are King of Rat and glory to the gulls.

Wood anemones slink through crumbs of soil,
heads bowed by darkness, darkness limned by toil.

JCBs shovel rancid rubbish over tilth.
They rule by ramming everything in sight.

Anemones explode like stars or solar flare.
They glow and glister on the forest floor.

JCBs chew up tonnage and spit out filth.
Magpies choose their JCB and stick by *him*.

Wood anemones shift sidelong to the sun.
Their shoots are metronomes in slow emotion.

Rooks erupt in raptures around a JCB.
Their Midas, Grail, their Holy of Holies.

Wood anemones harvest ultraviolet rays.
Early bees are drawn droning to their gaze.

Nothing saddens a JCB more than a stalled JCB.
He ploughs across the planet to hold him, steady.

The lives of wood anemones are swift. We hail
their fleet and fleetness, their golden crisis.

JCBs squat on fly-blown, bird-flocked hills.
Spring detonates on time, thanks to JCBs.

David Morley

Die Holzwege

*'the eye of the nihilist ... is unfaithful
to his memories: it allows them to drop,
to lose their leaves ...'*
– Friedrich Nietzsche

1

These woodland paths like arguments
about belonging here have rents
shot through with leaf-stopped rays
and shady undergrowth, tired ways
in a world of airborne ills where,
detached, we're still able to care
that Dutch elm, dieback, acid rain
find the woods in trouble ...

2

as when shivered fronds' foxed fringes
start awe in our ordinary exchanges
about more losses, and memories
like the leaves on deciduous trees
fall naturally ...

3

for even belonging's tainted now our
advocates of being, their will to power,
have appropriated woodland paths
leaving only an autumn's aftermaths;

you ask me if that beech is dead,
but I suppose it must have shed
leaves early, look, its shrivelled rust
carpet …

4

and how the tree survives on trust!

Peter Robinson

Final Memo from the Ministry

Tinted soda-lime, the windows' notice-board
shows many states of occupied withdrawal:
the forest vaults reconstituted from Hansard,
the muffled squares, the suffragan cathedrals

shady beneath the branches of Bastard Service.
Half the staff already gone –
Why? We were busy, busy in every office:
Sidney Street, Runnymede, Tyburn …

But we have officially outlasted our purpose.
And where we are to go, no one supposes.
Variegations of mosaic virus
have ruined our imported Paestum roses.

James Brookes

Love Poem with Beech Coppard

for Zac

Another heavy night,
the endless freight trains speeding past
and curtains leaking light...
I try to think about beechmast

we collected in the woods
on Saturday: those little shells
which crackled underfoot,
the tiny three-edged nut they held

so tight... But wake again...
And so I start to grow around
our room a veteran
of beech, the coppice from the ground

to nest our bodies, heads,
then a claw of ancient pollard
encircling the bed.
And while you sleep so fast and hard

I will attend the tree,
for birds, black beetles, bats, and keep
the dead wood turned, and see
it safe in storm. I too might sleep,

for what else but a crown
of thickset branches could protect
our limbs, grown so well known
that with a hug you now detect

this woodland I've conceived –
and pull me in against the fight,
to dream in just the leaves,
just woodland noise and woodland light.

Michael McKimm

Refuge

What washes up in the forest is no less
a wonder than the flotsam of oceans.

Take this skeleton of an upturned ark
stranded among a reach of ash trees,

beached in leaf litter, its ribs and spars
secured by a rigging of twiggy larch,

tangles of plaited honeysuckle, all
leaning in as though wanting to give ear

to silence, breathe the wood's cool must.
Some Crusoe surely built this, laid limbs

against a fallen ridgepole, wove vines
and brushwood, spread out a bed of brash,

learned how stillness is a state of mind,
here where things slither, drip and flinch.

Stephen Boyce

What Newton Didn't Notice

When you sit under a tree,
the truth of gravity will hit you,
even if an apple doesn't.
Here, you are earthed.

Walk for an hour in a wood
then let yourself be pulled down
by an oak, a fir, an ash.
Feel your weight on the ground

and the world will be explained to you:
dryness by the needles between your fingers,
memory by sycamore keys,
age by roots that refuse to be invisible.

Acorns will help you understand beginnings.
Light is what works its way in.
You will know luck if you hear a peewit
or see a blackbird, or if

a green beetle crawls over your boot.
And maybe you will notice that moss
is its own forest and you will wish
you were small enough to enter it.

Do this for an hour, find
you are still fixed and yet
floating. You have discovered levity,
and the patchy light has found you.

Ailsa Holland

Stand

I can say this space slowed me:
Bottleneck through bark on my old walk
To work, a clot of stood wooden tourists whose path–
Bending presence stayed me, could have made
Me one of their long number and dropped
My pace, my breath branching in air
As I wiped roots from my soles.

The wood outgrew the staked space
Of its elders, their penumbra, ghost of the storms
It was named for, made up for,
The sun behind me and trees – dodged
In the moment of shadow –
Now and at day's end level with land
To make barcodes of trunks.

The windscreens carry light below to the left of me
Speed day away from the city or strain
Eyes beaming it back to the east.
I turn from the air they pull, lose my footing
Take bark's fingerprint on my hand:
Our own mark is two decades in wood, the scatter
Of crowns scanned by the cloud-cutting jets
That are walking me into their wake.

The trees could not call my name, halt my
Going-being, any more than I read
Their different signatures picked out in light.
But in the lee of the wood a huge fallen trunk
Belatedly says to me 'wait' –

81

And I am stood myself at the edge of it,
The round of my green iris wanting
To hold it, to mean it, wondering
What I have left of me there as I stare.

Matthew Griffiths

The Audition

Unnamed Forest, Knotty Green

Backstage, past the tutus and wigs
brambled with berries, nettled gates,
horses cantering in legwarmers,
to a clearing.

It's still here, struck so long its face is crackling moss.

The lights adjust,
some unseen techie switching the gels.

The auditorium is too quiet – trees taut as strings
chuchotte in the wind.

This time, I've come alone.

I test the trunk with different legs.
Can I walk it? Right one thrown forward, toiled into a rond-
de-jambe, then an attempt at a penché.

And now? And now?
I feel the stretch, then tilt, leafwards.

Claire Trévien

Almost

You could lose yourself even now
in the wood's bewilderment, stalked at dusk
by that childhood story: the three of us
where the path divided, so one must split
off from the others to test a theory that
the track meets itself again, quite soon,
which is how it always looks to children,
both ways curving sweetly like brackets through
ferns and dog's mercury, friendly arms
around a tear-shaped spinney.
You'll remember

how it felt then to be the forest's only child,
tripping over roots in the twig-snapping silence,
mouth purple with juice, spooked by white
destroying angels, cracking unripe nuts for pale
kernels of hope – the path fading into somewhere
else.
In the wood's silent theatre, listen

to the subsong of birds, sapsong of oaks, sift
of generations of summers. First leaf falling.
Find yourself now in the heart's clearing,
this spell of no wind to speak of that has the year
on precarious hold, though leaves and the story
are no more still than your own breath and blood:
sense them trembling in the moment's balance
on an edge, the between of summer and winter,
yourself and the others, outset and homing.

Linda Saunders

84

Among the Birches

Among the birches it is purple; dim shade before me;
behind me, the surf sound of the city is receding
At my right hand I see the White Lady, at my left the Dark
Lad, Hogyn Ddu
The trees have so many half-heard songs, stories & voices,
half-seen names, faces & gestures skyward
Above me swaying, lacing fronds bend against the Winter
sodium night as it swells into the deep
& below me the roots recite neuropeptide sequences into
the network for transmission & storage further down.
Upon the birches, deep in mythic heath-night,
constellations of buds wait until the stars are due right,
Each like a coiled spring awaits the virid signal that will
free the strength of Summer now gone & to come again,
Filled with fossilised light. For now, they are the co-
ordinates of the wind as branches sigh & seethe in a black spray.
I lie down & forget what they are, forget their names,
their anatomical identity, hear only song;
Threads of water & sap vibrate like strings, fibres groan &
twist; scarred, pale bodies dance;
No moon, just the unearthly radiance of an urban wood
not so far from that gaudy, flickering rectangle,
I don't call this being alone, I call it home; suddenly the
wind drops & everything is perfectly still.
You can no longer see me & I no longer care, I hold my
breath awaiting the return of North-East winds
From the Taiga, from northern vastness, from the chaga
forests, alive with the calls of beasts which you
exterminated here long ago,
Root, branch & mycelial net are extensions of my our
body & ways of knowing & feeling you lost,
That you fear. But I am safer among the trees than in my
own street & they don't lie to me,

& the stories we share aren't for entertainment &
distraction they are maps of the world within, a molecule
is a thought but a thought is not a molecule.
Will you ever learn the language of the trees? Seek it in
your own blood, your own glands & get out here in the woods
To hear the ancient song sung by birds & by the wind
among the birches in the purple twig Winter.

Barry Patterson

The Greenwood

A nice idea, but no one is going to take to it
to escape the law, and what it offers isn't
a country of itself, complete with courts and fools.

There may be barbed wire and tracks made by heavy plant
used for hauling timber down to yards. There may be
sign-posted public rights of way for all abilities.

The Greenwood isn't what it used to be. But stand me
in a still, cold-folded clearing and I will see shades
of the old world, the dark, fierce freedom of trees.

Jonathan Davidson

PEOPLE

The Forests of South London

Shaggy acorn cups of Turkey oak mulch
the roots of chestnut, alder, willow, ash,
a fancy strain brought in for hardiness.
Over centuries they arrive, the introduced,
the invited, *continental* or *exotic*, useful maybe,
or like a breath of fresh air, *bohemian,*
and others, mere blow-ins, taking root,
scattering seed *right, left and centre.*
There have been more formal arrangements,
coppiced, pollarded, espaliered even, yet now
slim shoots, electric with their own beauty,
bend in the newest breeze and blossom.
See how our colours fill the summer streets,
the sweet strength of us massing and blooming.

Maura Dooley

Woods, and us

I grew up in a wood.
Well, no. I slept in bed
but spent my days by blackbirds. Rooks
cawed in my head.

I found the thrush's nest,
her cup of warm-pressed mud.
The beech trees straining to their light
sighed in my blood.

We never owned that place,
I moved at eight. And so
in town gardens, in narrowed space,
I watched trees grow

where sparrows shrilled, but neighbours
fretted for light or drains.
Now, many blackbirds later,
I find wide woods again

which few of us can grow
which no one truly owns,
new pine tips which flash red, long paths
dry as our bones.

The children storm high walks,
the broadest ground they know
beyond tall timbers, bird or fox,
our woods, where people grow.

Alison Brackenbury

Out of the Woods

for Lucian

The day we met I thought about
the trees I played in as a child;
leaves breaking into a canopy of green.
Already we're interweaving
branches, building a den,
finding that from sturdy roots
you can stretch and grow.
I can't wait for us to walk
among bluebells and discover
red admiral caterpillars, pick
berries straight from the bush.
In your limbs there's the strength
of great oaks – the capacity
to climb to the top.

Sally Flint

The New Term

I suppose it would have been dusk,
the car they were getting back into
facing in the wrong direction,

the girl with her arm wrapped
round me like a ribbon
a comfort to my parents at least.

When she leaned in close
and smiled, to tell me what
would happen once they'd left,

she'd got it wrong for once.
She didn't know that trees
were places to read letters,

hide invisible friends in,
that the forest – as per
the book – was indeed

my kingdom. She said
they'd make me climb
the tallest pine and leave

me there all night – it must
have been one in the eye for her
when I agreed.

Carolyn Oulton

Ash Tree

I

Six years old and soaked down to the skin,
no coat, and the valley gone heron-grey,
you remember the tree that edges the wood.

To squeeze in you must first stand sideways:
drop in one leg, then slide – jumper catching
on the lip of the bark – to the charcoal dark of the hollow.

Stillness. Silence. A continent's
shift in time and place.

Outside the rain slips down the valley:
plastic sheeting sliced. Astonishingly still,
the cows drop their heads in surrender.

From the brown thorns of the barbed wire fence
rain passes to the ground.

II

Hold on to this when the car alarms bark
and the traffic calls out in the night.

Hold this when the floor-boards contract,
and the kids or the heating or the bin men erupt.

Hold the liquorice dark of the wood;
the musk and sea-shore smell; the sieved red sand
of the floor; the crisp packets pushed into corners.

Hold the sense, as you sleep at last,
of the great wings of the branches and boughs,
spreading from beneath your shoulder blades up.

Hold the eagerness of spiders and beetles in the leaves.
The snowdrop bulb; the weevil's skin;
the movement of grass in the dray.

Hold the escapology of the nuthatch; the mite
in the crevice beneath the black crow's wing;
the old lady whiteness of that skin.

Hold the heft and plumb of the root,
thigh-thick and harder than stone; the great
spreading out and down, through the ancient bones of tractors.

Down through ampules and light bulbs;
down through pomegranate seeds of gravel;
the origami skull of the shrew.

To the threaded root-fibres of the brain, as if silk worms
had formed their own city.

Now, come back from the root, to the hollow, to the ash,
to the double-glazed windows of your home,
where your parents wait calmly in the kitchen,
the great brown block of the microwave humming.

Richard Evans

Harlow New Town

1

Ken and Gaynor's house is the last
in a street which feels as if it runs
into countryside. The tarmac ends
further up. Here, there are
playing fields opposite, seen
through a spinney bordered with blackthorn.
Perhaps part of the road name,
Blackbush Springs, derives from this.

Walking back with Odette from
The Stow, a shopping precinct,
I took a turn with that first pushchair.
It had been a welcome pass-down
though unwieldy, the more so
in my out-of-practice hands.
How pleasant on a hot day to step
into dappled shade. A country lane,
almost, native hedgerow
on either side and, underfoot,
a subtle change of texture from the urban.
Traces of puddles ringed with dried mud,
snapped twigs, fallen leaves, things
which only a tree canopy gives.
We came to their house as if upon
a cottage at a clearing in the woods.

2

Harlow was designated as
a New Town in 1947.
Frederick Gibberd's masterplan was strongly
influenced by the character
of the surrounding landscape, its hills,
valleys and woods. He structured
the town using blocks of woodland,
hedgerows and hedgerow trees
to act as green wedges which would
define the urban areas. The plan
provided for tree-planting on
a massive scale. Work began in 1950.

3

Do you remember that day, John? They were
still living with Odette's parents.
We walked into town with her, bought
shoes for her birthday and ended up
at that café with all the other mums
and buggies and dads and nans and grandads.
It turned out the woman who ran it came
from Istanbul and tried to teach you
some Turkish phrases. Do you remember?
It was the first time Odette had taken
Brinley in the pushchair all the way
into the town centre from Blackbush Springs.
We followed the path she said she'd liked using
when she was at college. True, there were
main roads to cross but we, too, liked
the sense of open space and natural green.

4

The Green Wedge Review of 2014
referred to an earlier local plan,
which described their role in much the way
Gibberd had originally intended.
They should separate housing clusters
from industry and retail, preserve
the town's natural features as habitats
for wildlife, whilst introducing
a rural character for the benefit
of people, and they should provide for
a range of informal recreation.
The Plan also noted that the Wedges
integrate with built-up areas best
'when they are maintained in a natural
or parkland state'. The Review
of 2014 went further.
New Green Wedges should include
woodland and allotments, as well as
orchards and community gardens.
It recognised the value of the smaller,
linear open spaces, in between
the Wedges. These are known as Green Fingers.

5

Before he knew Odette, Trevor used
to share a flat at Great Plumtree
in one of the original neighbourhoods,
built in the 1950s. The block
is low-rise and light, with a glazed
stairwell. To the rear is open green.
The frontage curves round to face the forecourt
as if to embrace the imposing tree standing
in the middle, a pleasure to observe

throughout the year from Trevor's window,
as well as being the focal point of the street.
Great Plumtree has weathered six
tough decades with grace. It's in
the Mark Hall Conservation Area.
No wonder Trevor couldn't afford, even
with help, to go on renting his place.

6

It was part of Gibberd's masterplan
to bring main roads into the town
buffered by green open land. With thorn
hedges on either side of the carriageway,
it feels like driving in the countryside.

Nell and I walked from the hotel
to the flat at Brays Mead shared
by her brother, Trevor, Odette
and their son, Brinley. Even though
the first part of the walk was on a main
road, Southern Way, and we were talking,
I couldn't help being aware of
the softening effect of dense foliage
running along beside us for a stretch.

If you look at a map of the town,
you will see that it is dotted with woods.
Some of these, such as Burnett's Wood
and Harold's Grove are classified as ancient,
many thousands of years old.
Anywhere in Harlow, you are never far
from green spaces and trees. Those planted
in Gibberd's time are now mature. Imagine
Latton Common with tethered horses,

wild flowers and, silhouetted
on the horizon, a line of lofty trees.

7

Other architects made contributions,
but The Lawn, Britain's first tower block,
is by Frederick Gibberd. Its nine storeys
stand on open ground, surrounded by oaks.

He wasn't one of those Modernists
who used their clientele as guinea pigs,
for a kind of housing they would never
live in themselves, then cleared off
to Hampstead. Gibberd designed his own
house and garden in Marsh Lane to the east.
He must have felt satisfaction, surely,
going in to change his library books
or take part in other activities
provided free by a Town Council
which has always worked to keep them so.
When he was walking round his creation,
did any residents recognise him?
He looked distinctive, all the more
in later life, his plentiful white hair.
What would they have said? Most people –
I have this from one of them – thought
they'd been born again in paradise,
being re-housed in Harlow New Town.

Vivien Freeman

Collins Guide to Trees

PAPERBACK Illustrated 1980.
Extensive creasing to the spine, pencil annotations.

Illustrations show the overall shape of the tree,
details of foliage, flowers, fruits and bark. Where you
have left a crease in the page we can feel them
in these lines made of trees lit at the speed of thought,
the tree that was growing before both of us.

*

A beginner's guide to identifying trees
native to Northern Europe is not the preferred condition,
the preferred condition is an understanding that is
like a slightly curled, bright yellow leaf in November,
somewhere between thick jacket weather and quick sun,
you holding a birch seed, demonstrating
the difference between the similar species
at a glance,
the difference between similar species,
because you dropped the first seed,
because you weren't 100%
looking.

*

There are deciduous and evergreen memories for both of us,
cousins wearing proud crowns, hoping the juices will run clear
without the knife going in – it's what makes you grow
vigorously – silence at the table broken by *Fuck! The broccoli!*

*

102

The life cycle of trees; the ash tree so majestic, bicycling
when no one is looking, or practising a speech, or
holding an owl up like the world cup.

★

Most people's relationships with forests are like the M6;
we would see the wood twice if we were lost, but rarely
one tree.
These woods could harbour criminals for all we know,
highwaymen who wanted a life outside the law,
who galloped from it all, raised kids, and since never left.
That's the kind of thing you would say,
holding this book in your hands like a Whitby jet necklace,
telling an audience all about this, and about the trees
about how macabre it is that you are contained by trees
trying to soak it all in, to talk your way in
with a mouthful of ink
into the real world where you live,
ranging from page to stage
organising homes in high eyries,
readying them for the latest origins of life.

Harry Man

Struck

The leaves aren't lit, but morning's struck a match
so I can see a path through Linacre – low gold
that spreads across the grates of reservoirs

and stokes the trees, long after an electric summer
and its short-fuse sky. September, sparking
on the ground so nobody can step into these woods

and not be burned. A woman calling for her dog
goes smouldering to moss. A cyclist
becomes a Catherine Wheel. I run

and feel my body catch, my face a taper,
shoulders taking light, my ribcage flammable.
I shed the new ash of my collarbones and spine

until I'm cinder, smoke, or left with all the parts
last winter made – the soft snow of my shoulders,
wrists and throat and when I try to hold

my voice I find it's thawed, a river,
all the names I ever knew
afloat.

Helen Mort

Tree, Bird, Plane, Cloud, Sky, Moon

If only I had my camera…

Fine, there was no plastic bag
to tag commercialism
absent was exhalation
from a choking industry
void it was, of skydiver in a suit
praying to his mother's god
for a backpack of pillows and dreams

Just: a base of a top of a tree, whole and layered;
a bird as it sifts currents with hollow bones;
a plane, tweaking tropopause with creaking frame;
Cash cloud and Coltrane sky – a default desktop theme
topped with a full moon at midday, cheating

Oh, how I wish I had a pic of this scene
to savour with a warming tumbler
whinge 'Oh the state of things'
crop onto my smartphone screen
forward to friends to share
in my sublime appreciation
of mystery, music, magic

If only I had my cam–
oh, there it is

Luigi Coppola

Laws For Trees

after I've identified my intention
to earn enough money and stay happy

there's the question: *how does this make you feel?*
and instantly I feel like a tree

leaves shot through with sun
roots zooming down into the good and loamy ground –

it's great being in here, all barked up and healthy,
I'm a functioning part of everything around

so strong I'll stay for as long as it takes
to persuade those screeching buzzards

to lay their eggs on my upper east side –
the wind has no discretion

it sticks its tongues in all my ears
till I'm rattled enough to remember

I live in a political community
and that's when I start soap-boxing

about refugees and equality
and how there's enough room for everyone –

my friend looks at me and I quote Octavio Paz –
a tree grows within and then

it's a Charlie Hebdo moment of the arboreal kind
je suis un chêne – I am an oak –

if I don't make it as a tree
I'll divert my energy into law

learn the language of the law-makers and defend
my arboreal friends until we've every successful

precedent we need: the case of Beech vs. Saw;
Oak vs. Saw; Elm vs. Saw; Maple vs. Saw

etc etc etc

Alyson Hallett

The boy who hurts trees

There's a tree with arms
uplifted, in supplication
or praise or, as a toddler
who lifts up his arms, obedient
to the mother who will come
to shimmy off his vest
or pyjamas; haul him
out of the cooled bath.

Tall and pale as a peeled tree himself,
he comes in the blank hours
of afternoons, before schools
have emptied, when only a woman
and her dog might cross
his path, eyes low,
scouring the ground.

Often he is weaponless,
using the might
of a steel-capped boot
to kick the tree, repeatedly,
till the bark ruptures.
Then he'll swing on a bough and make it sag,
twist and wrestle it to the ground
to leave a jagged stump.

But sometimes he'll take out a knife
and stab his tree, wounding the bark
till he's able to claw some off with his fingers.
Then, again with the knife, he'll hack
at the pulp, *Bad tree. That'll teach you.*

Boy, under what bed
do you lay your fine boots? In what drawer
do you close up your knives?
Between what sheets – if any – do you sheathe
that bare body of yours?

Elizabeth Cook

I Found a *Tree-jinn* in the Lake

> *'Jinn can be fiery spirits but while they are disruptive of human life,
> they are still considered worthy of being saved.'*
> – Encyclopedia Mythica

I found a tree-*Jinn* in the lake.
   I didn't know what was at stake.
I laid his body in my lap
   then tore away the filmy wrap

and made to kiss his mouth once more
   to give him life? – I wasn't sure.
He woke and flew into a tree,
   sodden he was – ruined with grief.

The boy had wild and shining eyes,
   he gave out such pitiful sighs.
His white face dazzled in the rain,
   marked by a variegated stain.

His lungs in shreds, his tongue ablaze,
   I tried to reach him with my gaze.
He glanced towards a branch that stirred
   and stretched to tap a burning bird

and when its perfume was released,
   I thought perhaps he'd find some peace.
His eyelids closed pale as death,
   nothing now but his ragged breath.

Tu baabis jaa – I whisper in fear
    and he begins to disappear...
his bluish fingers clasp the bark
    and he is absorbed in the dark.

And so as the night comes in,
    I make a gift of a bobby pin –
and lay the offering upon the ground
    as a leaf lands without a sound.

I wish I had intruded more –
    the marbles on the forest floor.
The boy gone now my body quailing
    and up above me tree-buds failing.

Mona Arshi

    Tu baabis jaa (Punjabi): Go back home.

100 mile drive to my father's care home

Last night with the thumb and fingers
of my right hand I held
a sprig of rosemary
by its freshly growing tip

and with the fingers and thumb
of my left I stripped it
into the pan till just a stalk remained
a few grey-green leaves on top

not quite cleanly skimmed
and every tree in this
flickering road-side pinewood plantation
imitates it

each tall stripped trunk
with half a dozen sprigs and twigs still live
up high and green
is scarred lower down and bare

and however much I try to hold them
these nearest pine trunks blur
my eyes fix only
on a random upright in the middle distance

before the movement
of the car strips out
even that speeding away my eyes jump/cut
light on a further grey trunk

steadied there for a few seconds
beyond the endless baffling foreground—
I hear crying *who are you*
who are you covering of dust

before the mirror old skin peeling back
layer on layer each day
as these dusty windscreens
suffer their rapid emptying

and re-filling their re-fuelling of light
from the cloudy impassive
bowl of sky that seems incapable
of remembering

Martyn Crucefix

The woman who loved trees

When I found I'd lost you –
not beside me, nor ahead,
nor right nor left nor
your green jacket moving
    – Kathleen Jamie, 'Glamourie'

The forest thinned
the summer you were gone,
huddled in thickets, corpses
thirsting for news

it was a dry month or three.
Twigs, unnamed, held
themselves up
against laminated sheets,

turned this way and that,
to find they were merely
syllables spoken by women
inert with daily busyness.

Healing all our jagged spaces,
you would find the heart in anything.

It was not his own disease
but you knew it was breaking him.
Some things are good for us,
but this a space too hard:

we avert our eyes and design
new attrition. The trees recolonize
our words rustle leaf mould
for envelopes that might hide you.

You only wanted light.
Can you see it play the silver birches
as we drive? I want to bottle, plait it,
felt it into woodland

to measure your heart and save it.

We are not veteran
but let us lay our elbows down and move

we will be lavish
          extravagant

          wasteful

          these human women, how they love .

Carol Rowntree Jones

Hurricanes are always given women's names

Donna, Carla, Katrina, Camille...

Perhaps it was a woman – the great gale.
No nameless Amazon pushing her shoulder
through boundaries to pick trees like flowers.

Nor an ageing dame disfiguring scapes
to make herself look better in the yellow light,
getting forests to dance with her all night.

But a composer of music too modern for the ear –
rushing in crescendos through tunnels
of branches, buckling symmetries, deliberate

in beheading crowns presiding for years.
Her thudding percussion demanding a hearing –
with so much to say, she needed a clearing

wider than autumns fluttering their last.
Was it deliberate: for a second – the suggestion
of napalm on wood burnt white like flesh

leaked into setts over the acorns' ammunition?
Such transgression: the skirts of every oak
yanked up with violence, pines once phallic

sudden stumps of impotence. Yet this was how
she warned against war; how she introduced
a timeless, fresh morning in which, a girl again,

she played – on treetops coated in mud –
with children who pressed, from beech crotches,
triangles of sky, collected off notches

her forgotten songs: secretive, genderless.
And gentle. Resin wept into felled trunks' rides;
batons once trees conducted the lull on all sides.

Donna, Carla, Katrina, Camille...
Only the ivy, hanging by itself in mid air,
bore telltale traces of maidenhair.

Patricia McCarthy

Melia (an ash tree spirit)

Winter

Girl–bud of ash birthed of blood in a
garden. Ash-bud of girl listening
in the school hall; listening for morning
music, to open her limbs.

Sweet green-worlds cradled between
leaf stalk and stem. Ash-bud of girl; tree-
cathedral, tree-city, in waiting.

Dog's mercury / mother's mercury
\\\\\ fallen, in transport,
from the woods, to the woods.

Ash-bud of left-girl, lost-girl, up-rooted,
she's collecting wands. Untended in
the garden, ears pressing bark for an answer.

★

Spring

A shieldless sleep, ash-bud wintered. Deer, rabbit,
hare and axe; kinks in her gnarled base. Drawn
by spring, stout and woody, grown against wind,
wishing, seedling to mulch, to be a tree.

A narrow fork weathers storms \\\\\
nest drowns – garden falls. Wakes,
mothering-ash-bud-of-girl, wakes, in
woodland shelter of sister-seedling.

Stunted-sister seedling   budding-ash of mothering-girl,
fight for light, fight for water, re-united. Un-nursed,
undisciplined. Stuffed with sugary treats. Unaided.
Racing roots & inner rot. Scales and aphids strike.

★

Summer

Mossy age trickles down, fertilising the young
& fungi will make powder of the body \\\\\
a tree of tiny pits and pustules saw
fear in bark-folds and wrinkles.

Ash-bud of girl   &   mother-bud of ash,
pink fresh-cut, turning blackhearted. In
the forest her crown sways above all.
Cleft, as if mouth. Crackles, as if burnt.

Sheds her crown to sleep before autumn
storms. Ash keys hang in air, ripening. Her
September store – others more taking than
giving, burnout. Ash-mother of buds, skin
lichen-green-refuge. Fostering
fungi, growing roots.

★

Autumn

Daughter-bud of ash-asleep, or not,
to waken, my hand sweats on
your shiverless door handle.

No axes, no storms.
Seedling ash straightens
under glass.

Slides on a skin,
ears and eyes.
Give seedlings forest air.

Ash-mother of buds
shower of oxygen
in the city park
streetlights force eternal summer
mountains, time, and axe spur growth.
I will risk hearing
wisdom before falling branches

★

Joanne Ashcroft

Poem of Leaves

I lie down in the leaves,
beneath me the earth.
I pull them over me
like a coat. I disappear
under the leaves
and sink into the earth
where I become one
with the place I am known
whose name has not forgotten
my name, place of rest,
place of leaves melting
into bone, the earth,
this earth, my coat,
with my name in it.

Anthony Wilson

Prisoner Writing Home

The view is open only so far
and does not include the sea.

Beside him, the bed
and a letter to his mother

or his father or his brother.
Does it matter?

There is one tree in the cell,
a thin sapling birch

that glints in the light
like church bells glint.

It has new buds coming –
he can smell the tang –

and such silent height
he's glad

to be merely a man.

All he can speak of
is the first true leaf

and the tree's good
capacity to grow

through concrete, towards
something it never claims

to understand.

Em Strang

View from a Manchester flat

My window looked onto other windows
a straight-line scene, bricks, metal, glass,
littered corners, a sleepless hum of cars
but there was, to make me smile,
a single slender tree, a birch,
its branches close enough
if I stretched beyond the sill
to touch.

This tree showed me seasons
swished its emerald shawl in spring,
in summer, framed my view
with dappled green. Blue tits pecked
for bugs, cocked their tiny heads
to view me, and sang, and flew,
and in winter, all clothes abandoned,
this tree etched its lacy dance
against the city grey.

One day, I came home and found it gone.
Sawdust and twigs, ignored discards,
and the hacked stump, a raw full stop
of life cut short.

My view became a question:
How could I tell my children's children
that once there were trees,
that we lost the birds?

Harriet Fraser

How the Light Filtered Through the Leaves

I have resisted forest thoughts for fear of finding
not a wilderness but only empty parking lots inside.

I should maybe clarify that, while the smell of pure pine is amazing,
I don't want my apartment to smell like Christmas all the time.

I see a woman with a stick of chalk, trying to remember leaves.
Only one shade of green, and oh, she should have looked.

The best-smelling candle I've ever owned (oh, how I miss it!)
runs to about $35 and smells exactly like the forest floor.

We deserve no more for what we have not husbanded.
Even this book, friends, even this book.

More New England smells would be great; I'm also curious
about candles that smell like Mediterranean trees/groves/woods

I've never carved my name into a living trunk
but there are trees that have imprinted me.

(umbrella pine, olive, lemon, etc.).
Something that also has earthy or woody notes would be optimal.

Orange, chestnut, poplar, mulberry. Mood lighting,
forest dusk, the creatures' chirp and scratch.

There's a candle I adore for this smell at Target for $15,
one of the crackly wick types. Comes in a huge jar, lasts forever.

A forest can't be carried in a matchbox in your pocket.
It is the opposite of that, though part of it.

The more natural and less perfumey the better.
Price-wise I'd like to stay under $25 a pop.

Isobel Dixon

They've No Time for Trees Today

She said there was a different attitude,
everyone was throwing away and no one
was mending. She loved walking
or driving in winter but never stopped
to observe for long, 'Oh look at the
Mountain Ash!' her sigh went up as she
booted past in the Mini and maybe I wasn't
looking either, only waiting to poke holes
in her snobbery, 'Wherever there were
Protestants, they planted trees!'
'And what about Spenser chopping them down
so he could kill every Gael? You could walk
from Cork to Limerick and not meet a soul
before the Plantation of Munster!' 'God,
you've an answer for everything, haven't you?'
'But I was only just saying!'
'And why can't we have a discussion?'
'Look you can still see the outline
of the carriageway to the front.
Imagine what we think is the front was
the back of the house then. It's all changed.'
She was right about the beeches,
meeting overhead on the road to Mallow –
a green gift from the planters. A lover
of funerals, she preferred Deanes' back
avenue past its heyday with its moss ruff
leading to the neglected cobbled yard,
ruined belfry, 'Servants, imagine it!'
The new bungalows were ugly.
'Oh I suppose people have to live somewhere'.
But trees were going to get scarcer because

'The people have gone stone mad!
A conservatory, three bathrooms and no one
inside in it, where will it end?'
'Sure what about the size of Deanes' House?'
'Well everyone can't be at it and that *is*
the size of it!' Only who gets to decide?
She was the one who, in the dark,
surreptitiously hacked down armfuls
of beech branches and stuck them
in the brown Victorian ewers
she'd rescued from Cotters', they blazed
emerald one summer in our cold salvaged
fireplaces, old was always good in her book.
She was always looking back
and now – me too, rooted,
staring after her.

Martina Evans

Mothers

Because when the croft tumbles its slow change into edges
and its walls and roof sink or split apart to love the
    landscape better –

to pull the hills and weather closer – and the hearth
    unbricks itself
and cools inside the sweep of fields, inside the reach of
    oldest sky,

the rowan that they planted will remain there, blooming
    its roots
like a second tree, flinging its outward reds and greens

against the spaces where a window was, and where a door
once opened into light. It safeguards only the foundations now,

of course – protecting nothing but the outlines of the house,
but holding fast and bodying each thing they knew to
    matter, nonetheless.

Because of this, perhaps, you bring a rowan spray and
    leave it in a vase.
Think better. Bring it closer. Put it for safekeeping in her hands.

Rachel Curzon

Committal

'We all need a second life, the one we have
goes spinning away too soon.'
– John Burnside, 'Nocturne: Christmas, 2012'

Today a teenage girl secured her right
to have herself cryonically preserved

so maybe in five hundred years or more,
once mutation's mystery has been solved,

her body may be warmed to stir again
and she can live the life she's barely led.

I also wish to carry on, here's how:
inter me deep in loamy woodland soil,

then plant a sapling oak above my head,
so hair and skin and bone may be reborn

in twig and leaf, in xylem, riddled bark;
so the seep of muscle and marrow may

replenish soil, feed worm and ant and moth…
and moth feed shrew and shrew feed owl and fox.

No need for messages carved into stone,
Your journey to the spirit world starts here –

just let the faintest hints of musk remain:
that pulse and trace of what we must become.

Andy Brown

The Acacia

On that corner near the Italian restaurant
where the road curves round to go west,

there's a tree stump, four to five feet high,
all last winter as dead, metallic as a bollard,

pruned back to a blunt fist of lifelessness; they
might as well have dug it up, have done with it.

Then one spring morning, I was stopped in my tracks
by it sparkling with light green shoots, a cascade of

sherbet lime fronds bursting around its butchered neck.
Take that, you bastards, it yelled, frenzied with its

own power and beauty, just take that. The next week
it was a silent stump again, sprigs hacked off. All winter

still I pass it every day, can sense it plotting under
its arid brown scales. Try and stop me, it's thinking.

Mary Woodward

Notes on Contributors

Simon Armitage is a poet, novelist, playwright, broadcaster, non-fiction writer and translator. He has published eleven collections of poetry, most recently *The Unaccompanied* (Faber & Faber). In 2015 he was appointed Professor of Poetry at Oxford University, and lives in Yorkshire.

Mona Arshi was born and still lives in London. She worked as a Human rights lawyer before she became a poet. Her debut collection *Small Hands* was published by Pavilion Poetry, part of Liverpool University Press, and won the Forward Prize for best first collection in 2015.

Joanne Ashcroft's first pamphlet *From Parts Becoming Whole* was published by Knives Forks and Spoons Press in 2011. She won the Poetry Wales Purple Moose competition in 2013, published as the pamphlet *Maps and Love Songs for Mina Loy* (Seren). She is a postgraduate research student at Edge Hill University where she also teaches poetry.

Jean Atkin has published *Not Lost Since Last Time* (Oversteps Books) as well as pamphlets and a novel. Her poems have won various prizes and recent work appears in *Magma*, *Envoi*, *The North*, *Earthlines* and *The Moth*. She works as a poet on education and community projects. www.jeanatkin.com

D.M. Black is the author of *Why Things Matter: the place of values in science, psychoanalysis and religion* (Routledge 2011). He has published a selection of translations of Goethe and six collections of poetry, most recently *The Arrow-maker* (Arc, 2017). www.dmblack.net.

Stephen Boyce lives in Dorset. A prize-winning poet, he is the author of two full length collections, *Desire Lines*

(Arrowhead 2010) and *The Sisyphus Dog* (Worple 2014), and two pamphlets, *In the Northland* and *Something Persists*. He is a founding trustee of Winchester Poetry Festival. www.stephenboycepoetry.com

Alison Brackenbury was born in Lincolnshire in 1953. Her ninth collection is *Skies* (Carcanet, 2016). This featured in *The Guardian*, *The Independent* and on Radio 4's *Front Row*, and was chosen as one of *The Observer's* Poetry Books of the Year. New poems can be read at her website: www.alisonbrackenbury.co.uk

James Brookes was born in 1986 and grew up in rural Sussex. He was an Eric Gregory Award winner in 2009 and his first full length poetry collection, *Sins of the Leopard,* was shortlisted for the 2013 Dylan Thomas Prize. He teaches English at Haileybury College in Hertfordshire.

Andy Brown is Professor of English and Creative Writing at Exeter University. His latest publications are the edited volumes *A Body of Work: Poetry & Medical Writing* (Bloomsbury, 2016) and *The Writing Occurs as Song: a Kelvin Corcoran Reader* (Shearsman, 2014), along with the poetry collections *Exurbia* (Worple Press, 2014) and *Watersong* (Shearsman, 2015).

Judy Brown's *Crowd Sensations* (Seren, 2016) is a Poetry Book Society Recommendation. Her first book, *Loudness* (Seren, 2011), was shortlisted for the Forward and Fenton Aldeburgh prizes for best first collection. Judy was Poet-in-Residence at the Wordsworth Trust in 2013 and a 2014 Writer-in-Residence at Gladstone's Library. She has won the Manchester Poetry Prize, the Poetry London Competition and the Templar Pamphlet Competition. www.judy-brown.co.uk

Elizabeth-Jane Burnett's poetry includes *oh-zones* (Knives, Forks and Spoons Press), *Rivering* (Oystercatcher Press) and *Swims* (Penned in the Margins). She curates ecopoetics exhibitions and is Senior Lecturer in Creative Writing at Newman University, Birmingham. Her forthcoming book, A Dictionary of the Soil, is supported by Penguin/Random House's WriteNow.

Ruth Calway is Anglo-Welsh and lives in the Brecon Beacons. This is the landscape that inspires her poetry and prose. She has taught creative writing, has worked in garden design and animal rescue, and ran her own arboricultural business for ten years with a particular interest and belief in ancient woodland conservation.

Peter Carpenter is co-director of Worple Press; the chapbook *Peace Camp* (Maquette, 2015) is the most recent of seven poetry collections; his work has appeared and been favourably reviewed in journals including the *TLS*, *Poetry Ireland* and *Poetry Review*. He is currently writing a book on David Bowie.

Gillian Clarke was National Poet of Wales 2008–2016. Awarded the Queen's Gold Medal for Poetry 2010, the Wilfred Owen Award 2012. Recent publications: *Selected Poems* (Picador, 2016) and, as co-editor, *The Map and the Clock, poems from Britain and Ireland,* (Faber, 2016). "How to Take Apart a Tree" is published in *Zoology*, forthcoming from Carcanet Press in 2017.

John Wedgwood Clarke is a poet, prose non-fiction writer and lecturer who regularly collaborates on interdisciplinary projects with artists, curators and scientists. His first collection *Ghost Pot* was published in 2013 and his new collection *Landfill* will be published by Valley Press in 2017.

Elizabeth Cook is a poet and fiction-writer, brought up in rural Dorset and now living in East London and Suffolk. She has often enjoyed the hospitality of trees and would like to reciprocate. *Bowl* (2006 & 2013) is published by Worple Press. A pamphlet of her new poems, *The Sound of the Rain,* will be published by The Garlic Press in 2017.

Swithun Cooper's poems have appeared in *Magma, Poetry London, The London Magazine, The Economist*'s arts magazine *Intelligent Life* and several anthologies. He won an Eric Gregory Award in 2009. He lives in London, where he works as a research librarian.

Luigi Coppola teaches and writes in London, England. Poems have appeared in: *Acumen, Anon, Equinox, Fourteen, The Frogmore Papers, Gold Dust, Ink, Sweat and Tears, Iota, Lighten Up, Magma, The Ofi Press, Orbis, Other Poetry, Pennine Platform, Poetry Digest, The Rialto, THE SHOp, Snakeskin, South, Strange Poetry* and *Stride Magazine.* www.luigicoppolapoetry.blogspot.co.uk

Martyn Crucefix's recent publications include *The Time We Turned* (Shearsman, 2014), *A Hatfield Mass* (Worple Press, 2014) and *Daodejing – a new version in English* (Enitharmon, 2016). Forthcoming new collection is *The Lovely Disciplines* (Seren, 2017) and a chapbook, *O. at the Edge of the Gorge* (Guillemot Press, 2017). www.martyncrucefix.com

Rachel Curzon was born in Leeds in 1978, and now lives and teaches in Hampshire. She was a recipient of an Eric Gregory Award in 2007, and her pamphlet was published in 2016 under the Faber New Poets scheme.

Jonathan Davidson is a poet – most recently *Early Train* (Smith/Doorstop, 2013) and *Humfrey Coningsby* (Valley Press, 2015) – and a radio dramatist – most recently *#Humfrey*

Coningsby (BBC Radio 4, 2015). He lives in the English Midlands and his favourite tree is the Beech.

Isobel Dixon's fourth collection *Bearings* is published by Modjaji in South Africa and Nine Arches in the UK, with re-issues of *A Fold in the Map* and *The Tempest Prognosticator* due in 2017. Her pamphlet, *The Leonids*, is published by Mariscat.

Maura Dooley's most recent collection of poetry is *The Silvering*. She teaches at Goldsmiths, University of London and is a Fellow of the Royal Society of Literature.

Peter Kane Dufault (1923–2013) grew up in Westchester County, N.Y., and studied at Harvard. He was variously employed as tree-surgeon, journalist, teacher, house-painter, pollster and, in 1968, he was a Liberal Party candidate for US Congress. Worple Press published *Looking in All Directions: Selected Poems 1954–2000* (2000) and *To Be in the Same World* (2007).

Jonathan Edwards's first collection, *My Family and Other Superheroes* (Seren) received the Costa Poetry Award and the Wales Book of the Year People's Choice Award. It was shortlisted for the Fenton Aldeburgh First Collection Prize.

Martina Evans was born in County Cork, the youngest of ten children. A poet and novelist, she is the author of eleven books of prose and poetry. Her latest collection is *The Windows of Graceland: New and Selected Poems*, published by Carcanet in 2016.

Richard Evans grew up in the Staffordshire Moorlands. He attended Leicester then Bristol University and now teaches English and Creative Writing in Kent.

Suzannah Evans grew up at the edge of the Wyre Forest in Worcestershire, and now lives in Sheffield where street trees are under threat from the City Council. She has published one pamphlet of poetry, *Confusion Species*, which was a winner in the 2011/12 Poetry Business Book and Pamphlet Competition.

Sally Flint has published two poetry collections: *Pieces of Us* (Worple Press) and *The Hospital Punch* (Maquette Publications). Her poems have been widely published and anthologised, most recently in *A Body of Work* (Bloomsbury). She lectures in creative writing and is a tutor with The Poetry School.

Harriet Fraser writes about environment and culture, blending documentary, interviews and community gatherings with solitary walking. She works collaboratively with her husband, photographer Rob Fraser, as *somewhere-nowhere*. Trees are at the centre of her recent project *The Long View*, which focuses on seven remarkably ordinary Cumbrian trees. www.thelongview.today

John Freeman's most recent books are *What Possessed Me* (Worple Press), and *Strata Smith and the Anthropocene* (Knives Forks and Spoons Press), both 2016. His earlier collections include *A Suite for Summer* (Worple), and *White Wings: New and Selected Prose Poems* (Contraband). He taught for many years at Cardiff University.

Vivien Freeman is a published novelist, prize-winning poet, one of the co-founders of Ware Poets, and an experienced Creative Writing teacher. She is a script reader with a leading agency and lives in the Vale of Glamorgan. *Rose Alleyn*, a novel set in 1900, will be published in 2017.

John Greening's recent collections include *Heath* (with Penelope Shuttle) and *To the War Poets* (Carcanet). His

Egyptian memoir, *Threading a Dream*, appears in 2017. A Bridport Prize winner, recipient of the Cholmondeley Award, *TLS* reviewer, and Eric Gregory judge, he is RLF Writing Fellow at Newnham College, Cambridge. 'Tree Rings' first appeared in the *TLS*. www.johngreening.co.uk

Matthew Griffiths is the author of the poetry collection *Natural Economy* and the pamphlet *How to be Late*; his critical book *The New Poetics of Climate Change* is published by Bloomsbury this summer. Other, made-up trees feature in his science-fiction novel *The Weather on Versimmon*.

Philip Gross is a poet, novelist and keen collaborator across art forms – most recently with Valerie Coffin Price, on *A Fold In The River* (Seren, 2015). *The Water Table* won the T.S. Eliot Prize 2009. A new collection, *A Bright Acoustic*, appears from Bloodaxe in June 2017.

Alyson Hallett's latest poetry pamphlet is *Toots* (Mariscat Press, 2017). She has also co-written a book with Phil Smith, *Walking, Stumbling, Limping, Falling* (Triarchy Press, 2017). She lives in Somerset, plays piano and takes migrating stones around the world. www.thestonelibrary.com

Lesley Harrison lives in the north-east of Scotland. Her poetry and prose examine how we locate ourselves in our landscape, and how landscape creates a sense-of-self. Her next collection, *Blue Pearl*, will be published by New Directions (NY) in July 2017.

Ailsa Holland is an award-winning poet who has been published in various journals (*Under the Radar, Angle, Nutshell, And Other Poems, Ink Sweat & Tears*) as well as in anthologies including *MAP: Poems After William Smith's Geological Map of 1815* (Worple, 2015) and *The Very Best of 52* (Nine Arches, 2015). Ailsa is the Director of Moormaid Press.

Michael Laskey co-founded and directed the Aldeburgh Poetry Festival through its first decade. He also co-edited fifty issues of the poetry magazine *Smiths Knoll*. He has published five collections, most recently *Weighing the Present* (Smith/Doorstop, 2014).

Harry Man's first pamphlet, *Lift,* won the UNESCO Bridges of Struga Award, and he was recently a Clarissa Luard Wordsworth Trust Poet in Residence. His latest pamphlet, *Finders Keepers,* about endangered species, was created in collaboration with the artist Sophie Gainsley. You can find more of his work at www.manmadebooks.co.uk

Patricia McCarthy is the editor of *Agenda* poetry journal (www.agendapoetry.co.uk). She won the National Poetry Competition 2013. Recent collections are: *Rodin's Shadow* (2012), *Horses between our Legs* (2014) and *Letters to Akhmatova* (2015). Forthcoming collections in 2017 include *Rockabye* (Worple Press), a new collection for battered women, and *Shot Silks* (Waterloo Press).

Michael McKimm is an Eric Gregory award winning poet. He is the author of *Still This Need* (Heaventree Press, 2009) and *Fossil Sunshine* (Worple Press, 2013), and the editor of *MAP: Poems After William Smith's Geological Map of 1815* (Worple Press, 2015). www.michaelmckimm.co.uk

Matt Merritt has published four collections of poetry, the latest being *The Elephant Tests* (Nine Arches Press, 2013), and his nature memoir, *A Sky Full Of Birds*, was published by Rider Books in 2016. He lives in Warwickshire, works as the editor of *Bird Watching Magazine,* and blogs at polyolbion.blogspot.co.uk/

Helen Moore is an award-winning British ecopoet and socially engaged artist based in NE Scotland. Her two poetry collections are *Hedge Fund, And Other Living Margins* (Shearsman Books, 2012) and, acclaimed by John Kinsella as "a milestone in the journey of ecopoetics", *ECOZOA* (Permanent Publications, 2015). 'Tears I Shed...' first appeared in *Plum Tree Tavern*. www.natures-words.co.uk

Andrew Motion was UK Poet Laureate from 1999–2009 and now teaches at Johns Hopkins University. He lives in Baltimore.

David Morley won the Ted Hughes Award for New Poetry in 2016 for *The Invisible Gift: Selected Poems* and a Cholmondeley Award in the same year for his contribution to poetry. His Carcanet collections include *The Magic of What's There*, *The Gypsy and the Poet*, *Enchantment*, *The Invisible Kings* and *Scientific Papers*.

Helen Mort has published two poetry collections with Chatto & Windus. Her first novel is forthcoming. She is a lecturer in creative writing in the Manchester Writing School at Manchester Metropolitan University.

Grace Nichols has received several awards for her poetry including The Commonwealth Poetry Prize, The Guyana Poetry Prize and a Cholmondley Award. Among her published books are: *I Is A Long-Memoried Woman*, *The Fat Black Woman's Poems* and *Picasso, I Want My Face Back*. Her newest collection is *The Insomnia Poems* (Bloodaxe, 2017).

Jeb Loy Nichols is an American-born singer, songwriter, musician, and artist currently living in Mid Wales. His series of prints *Trees I've Planted* celebrated 2000 broadleaf Welsh natives he planted on his land. His latest album is *Country Hustle*. www.jebloynichols.co.uk

Carolyn Oulton is a Professor of Victorian Literature and Director of the International Centre for Victorian Women

Writers, at Canterbury Christ Church University. Her publications include biographies of Mary Cholmondeley and Jerome K. Jerome and her most recent poetry collection, *Accidental Fruit*, is published by Worple Press.

Barry Patterson is a writer and performer living in Coventry in the West Midlands. His alter ego, the Wild Man of the Woods, is Britain's widest travelled & longest running green man performance. His collection *Nature Mystic* was published by Heaventree Press in 2008. He is currently the Poet Laureate of Wroth Silver, one of the oldest continuously recorded public ceremonies in England. www.redsandstonehill.net

Mario Petrucci is an award-winning poet, ecologist and PhD physicist. He has held poetry residencies at the Imperial War Museum and with BBC Radio 3. *Heavy Water: a poem for Chernobyl* (Enitharmon, 2004) won the Daily Telegraph/ Arvon Prize. *i tulips* (Enitharmon, 2010) exemplifies Petrucci's distinctive combination of innovation and humanity. 'beetles' first appeared in *Poetry Wales*. www.mariopetrucci.com

Kate Potts is a London-based poet and creative writing lecturer. Her first full-length collection is *Pure Hustle* (Bloodaxe). Kate teaches for Oxford University, Royal Holloway, and The Poetry School. She is co-director of site-specific poetry organisation *Somewhere in Particular* and is currently completing a PhD on the poetic radio play.

Peter Robinson has published aphorisms, short stories, literary criticism and many books of poetry and translations, for some of which he has been awarded the Cheltenham Prize, the John Florio Prize and two Poetry Book Society Recommendations. Recent books include the novel *September in the Rain* (2016) and *Collected Poems 1976–2016* (2017).

Carol Rowntree Jones won the inaugural Overton Poetry Prize with her sequence *This Is Not Normal Behaviour*, published by Lamplight Press. Her work has also appeared in *The North*, *Staple*, *Assent* and *1110*. She has a chapbook out with Dancing Girl Press in the US.

Linda Saunders has been widely published in magazines and anthologies, including *New Women Poets* from Bloodaxe Books. Her fourth book, *A Touch on the Remote*, was published in 2016 by Worple Press. Her first full-length collection was short-listed for the Jerwood Aldeburgh Prize.

Joanna Seldon (neé Pappworth) was brought up in South Hampstead and studied English at Oxford. Joanna wrote three novels and several short stories, all of which can be found on her website. She was diagnosed with an incurable cancer in 2011, and lived with it bravely for five and a half years until her death at the end of 2016. Her collection *The Bright White Tree* was published by Worple Press in 2017.

Penelope Shuttle lives in Cornwall. Her eleventh collection, Will You Walk A Little Faster? was published by Bloodaxe in May 2017. *Heath* (with John Greening), their exploration of Hounslow Heath, appeared in July 2016 (Nine Arches Press). A pamphlet, *Four Portions of Everything on the Menu for M'sieur Monet!* was published in August 2016 (Indigo Dreams Publications).

Ben Smith is a Lecturer in Creative Writing at Plymouth University. His first chapbook, *Sky Burials*, was published by Worple Press. He is on the editorial team of *The Clearing* and is the co-organiser of *Crosscurrents*, an interdisciplinary project bringing together poets and marine scientists. He lives in North Cornwall.

Em Strang is a poet, editor and prison tutor. Her writing preoccupations are with 'nature', spirituality and the relationship between the human and nonhuman. Her illustrated pamphlet, *Stone*, was published in March 2016 by Atlantic Press with all proceeds going to Scottish charity, Trees For Life. *Bird-Woman*, her first full collection, was published by Shearsman in October 2016. She's currently working on a novella.

Paul (Abdul Wadud) Sutherland, a British-Canadian poet, emigrated from Canada in 1973. He has published eleven collections including *New and Selected Poems* (Valley Press, 2016). He founded the journal *Dream Catcher*. He's appeared in magazines, anthologies and read in public many times. He turned freelance 2004 and became a Sufi Muslim. He lives in Lincolnshire with his wife.

Claire Trévien is the author of *The Shipwrecked House* (Penned in the Margins, 2011), and *Astéronymes* (Penned in the Margins, 2016). She founded Sabotage Reviews and its annual indie literature awards. www.clairetrevien.co.uk

Anthony Wilson is a poet, writing tutor, blogger and Senior Lecturer at the Graduate School of Education, University of Exeter. His most recent books are *Lifesaving Poems* (Bloodaxe, 2015), *Riddance* (Worple Press, 2012) and *Love for Now* (Impress Books, 2012). He lives and works in Exeter and blogs at www.anthonywilsonpoetry.com

Mary Woodward has published one pamphlet – *Almost like Talking* (Smith/Doorstop, 1993) – and one collection – *The White Valentine* (Worple Press, 2014), which was highly commended in the Forward Prize 2014. She is the winner of the Barn Owl Trust poetry competition 2016 and the Guardian Jackie Moore prize for fashion journalism 2003.

William Wootten's poetry collection *You Have a Visitor* is published by Worple Press. His poems have appeared in magazines including *Poetry Review*, *PN Review*, the *Spectator*, and the *Times Literary Supplement*.

Thanks

Enormous thanks to the poets included in this anthology, for their generosity and enthusiasm, their time and energy, for responding so whole heartedly to the Charter for Trees and for their fantastic poems. And thanks so much to Jeb Loy Nichols for the stunning cover image.

I am grateful to Peter and Amanda Carpenter for inviting me to edit this anthology, and for their support throughout the project.

We are grateful to the Legal Sustainability Alliance for supporting the anthology and to the Woodland Trust, particularly Matt Larsen-Daw, for welcoming us as part of the Tree Charter initiative.

Finally, my biggest thanks to Zachary Lamdin, for walking with me in the woods, planting saplings, and helping to shuffle the leaves.

Michael McKimm